SWEET DREAMS. . .

BITTER AWAKENINGS

To Tom and Beth Holden —
May Your Sweet Dreams
come true —
Always !

Pat

by
PATRICIA A. LIVELY

LIVELY PUBLICATIONS
7925 King Road
Spring Arbor, MI 49283

ISBN 1-889808-00-8
Library of Congress Catalog Card Number: 96-94676

Photography by Mel Lively
Layout and Design by Leisa Meggison
Printed and bound in the United States of America

~ ACKNOWLEDGMENTS ~

The material in this book is either derived from my own observation or taken from official records or is the result of interviews with the persons directly concerned. Some of the "collaborators" are identified within the text. I want to express my gratitude to them, and thank certain persons who made specific contributions to my work.

I will start at the beginning with my husband Mel, who encouraged and supported the idea when I first mentioned the possibility of this book. Special recognition goes to our daughter Leisa Meggison, my unofficial editor, for the layout and design. And especially to Kirk Tabbey for his contribution to this story. Tabbey was gracious and helpful and put me in touch with the right people. Thanks to Detective Sgt. Mark Siegel who assisted the investigation as well as the prosecutors and Judge Charles Nelson who sentenced Marsha Denman.

On behalf of the victims, I wish to pay recognition to Carole France for the mental and physical stability she displayed in assisting the investigation and for her contribution to this story.

I wish to thank Spring Arbor College Professor Dr. Wally Metts, who motivated my desire to succeed and urged me to attain higher goals; Roy Meador, Library Director at Spring Arbor College and Betty Lathrop, Instructor at Baker College for their unconstrained expertise and instruction.

A special thanks to the Jackson District Library staff, who selected and held material, thus saving time in my busy life. Also, to the Creative Writing classes at Spring Arbor College and the Writer's Workshop members who listened patiently and suggested openly, especially Fred Bruey and Dorothy Graham.

To Ken Wyatt, for his assistance in legal and editorial matters. To Scott Davis, for sharing his gentle but firm commitment to produce accurate, interesting journalism.

At Chapter Thirteen, my computer hiccuped, locked up and crashed. Thanks to Johnny Eiler, the talented and helpful computer whiz who came to my rescue, scanned and recovered my lost words. To his dad, "Big John," who provided CD music for the writer's ear.

To the managers and waitresses at Cracker Barrel Restaurant for their encouragement and the never-ending cup of coffee as I revised and edited.

And to you, the reader, may all your dreams be fulfilled.

~ *FOREWORD* ~

The purpose of this book is not to add to the desperation or create attitudes for or against the defendant or persons involved on her behalf. It is a story about how the crime affected the victims. How they viewed the process. How the case worked as it lurched through the court systems. How average people dealt with the anxiety, frustration and humiliation produced by circumstances beyond their control.

The story is based on real incidents. Information provided by others and quotations taken from public records were verified, and every effort has been made to report them accurately. The account of events is limited only by the author's powers of description and interpretation.

~ About the Author ~

Pat Lively and her husband Mel share their retirement in a ranch home located in a small town in Michigan. Pat, who is as lively as her name, enjoys an interesting and diverse life.

Following closely behind her love for family and friends is a special love for music, having been involved with several musical groups, choirs and Spring Arbor College ensembles. Pat, her husband, son, daughter and other musicians and singers have recorded songs she composed and performed in churches, auditoriums and festivals. She currently studies music with the highly respected Spring Arbor College instructor, Monte Long.

Along with writing for magazines and newspapers, she also enjoys writing fiction, poetry and especially children's books.

Pat enjoys participating in the Jackson Civic Theater, has studied public speaking and serves as mistress of ceremony for musical concerts and various women's groups. She often assists her husband as a freelance photographer.

Her next project, "Patty's Promise," is an auto-biography in which she writes with great discernment about some of life's joys, fears, death and disappointments. Her struggles for answers sometimes result in humor and pleasure.

~ CONTENTS ~

~ CHAPTER ONE ~

THE DREAM

Outside, it was a sunny June afternoon. Inside, a picture-perfect buffet table displayed colorful summer fruits, crisp garden vegetables, mouth-watering potato salad, cold cuts and savory meat balls. A cherry chip cake topped with a ceramic bride and groom was displayed on a raspberry table cloth. Vivid teal and raspberry complemented the decor, which included a money tree with a suggestion that it be used next summer to help my husband Mel and me fulfill a dream—an Alaskan cruise.

I was like a brand-new bride in a white crocheted dress that I had purchased to take on the cruise. Musical equipment set up in the spacious church fellowship hall provided the opportunity to sing to Mel, still handsome and tall, in a blue-gray suit which complemented his silver hair.

All my hopes and all my dreams were suddenly fulfilled,
It's almost unbelievable, that you were in His will,
And only God could love you more than I do.

The touch of his hand created a sparkle in my eyes as we lifted a toast glass to the voices in unison, "Happy Thirty-fifth Anniversary."

Our blended family consists of two daughters, two sons and nine grandchildren. Our daughter Leisa, and her husband Mike organized a memorable day. Mike ran errands, helping wherever needed, while caring for two-year-old Josh, whose blue eyes and ready smile are like his mom's. Nathan, their seven-year-old blond, blue-eyed son entertained his cousins with jokes and guessing games.

It was a thrill indeed when our son Gary and his wife Teri added to the family's female population, thus granting us the pleasure of seeing patent leather shoes and frilly dresses among the grandsons' tennis shoes and jeans. Three-year-old Lauren has Goldilock's curls and a soft lyrical voice and petite Lindsay recently celebrated her first birthday.

Friends and relatives came from several different states. We shared stories and recalled memories of special fun times. I opened a gift from Dorothy, our matron of honor, and her husband Burt. She read the words from a wall plaque:

> *There's a miracle called Friendship which dwells*
> *within the heart. And you don't know how it happens or*
> *where it gets its start. But the happiness it brings you,*
> *always gives a special lift, And you realize that Friend-*
> *ship, is God's most precious gift.*

Without a doubt, I correctly labeled a duo of vivacious, witty bridesmaids, my niece, Joy Naylor and Lois Washburn, as the instigators of daring amusement. Lois composed and read a poem about their fun and games.

> *Your wedding day in June, we remember it well.*
> *Ah, yes, we remember. Many stories to tell,*
> *Like your first apartment. We found it that day,*
> *Spruced it up, and were on our way.*
> *Cotton-ball road led to the bedroom door.*
> *Removed can labels, sprinkled rice on the floor.*
> *We hung Pat's aged girdle on the hallway door.*
> *Living room furniture rearranged, and more.*
> *Hangers in the bed, pins and such,*
> *We tried very hard to add our special touch.*
> *Then hurried on back to join the party,*

Lest we leave the impression that we were tardy.
We all stood around, tried to look sad.
As you opened your card, you knew you'd been had.
We signed a sympathy card, gave it to you that day.
You both laughed hard. We wondered what you'd say.
All this is behind you. Your anniversary is here.
We're glad for your happiness the past thirty-five years.

I told our guests, "We returned from our honeymoon and saw how much they had spruced up the apartment. We wondered how our six attendants could do so much raillery in just fifteen minutes without being missed at the reception. Three months later, I found a bra in the freezer."

Leisa summarized our special day. "Love is the most important thing in the world. Equally important is friendship. Thank you for giving us both. You are all like family," she said with a smile.

The celebration was lovelier than I had ever dreamed. Expressions of love renewed memories of our wedding day, Saturday, June 6, 1959. The minister's announcement, "I pronounce you husband and wife," completed my girlhood dream of a white satin dress with long pointed sleeves, lace and pearls and my brown-eyed, handsome groom. I chuckled while recalling that on that day, Mel had discovered the tuxedo trousers were size 48 instead of size 32. He and the best man, his brother Harold, pinned them several times. The tailor's mistake was covered by the jacket and cummerbund.

The wedding reception was held in a Nazarene church dining room which utilized circular fans as a cooling system. We soon regretted our decision to spend hours opening beautifully wrapped gifts in 92 degree heat rather than accepting help from the bridal party. As we left for a northern Michigan honeymoon Mel said, "Someday we'll celebrate our anniversary with an Alaskan cruise."

After Mel retired, he looked forward to the daily visit to the mailbox and a friendly smile from Harriet Videto, our prompt, efficient and marvelous mail lady. Her blond hair and friendly blue eyes complement a winsome smile. She's an easygoing individual with a natural sense of humor. Her height allows her left foot to stretch to accommodate the brake and gas pedal on her gray Chevrolet's frequent mail stops. I've been tempted to ask, "When you stand, is your left leg longer than the right?"

In October 1993, two business associates told Mel and me that our local college president had become aware of, and helped set up, what appeared to be a wonderful vacation opportunity—an Alaskan cruise. Several people in the community had previously taken trips arranged by Marsha Denman's Network Discount Travel Service. Many had paid their money as long as two years before my inquiry.

Among the information they shared was a receipt for Alaska's inside passage. Included in the cost was airline fare to Vancouver and return, lodging for one night prior to sailing and a seven-day, six-night cruise. Individuals with whom we checked had only positive information about Marsha. We were assured that she had fulfilled promises in every respect.

I called Marsha on December 1, 1993, and made reservations for July 15, 1994, prime time, at an *unbelievably* low price of $1,450 per couple. She said the ship would send a receipt, a questionnaire, a booklet and that the 350 people from our area will be booked on the same deck.

Our dreams included expectations of viewing glorious glaciers surrounded by some of the tallest mountains in North America, beautiful waterfalls and abundant marine wildlife. Since we had previously cruised the Caribbean, we looked forward to the tantalizing cuisine served on crisp white linen, sparkling crystal, fresh-cut flowers and the lights turned low as shimmering candles create a romantic dining experience.

The next week I called Marsha to verify that my facts were correct regarding the overnight stay in Vancouver. "The cost is so low. Is this a good hotel?" I asked.

She assured me, "It is a first class hotel in modern Vancouver, Canada's third largest city with a European feeling, but a personality all its own. There are a lot of beautiful parks, and you'll have plenty of time to take tours including Chinatown and Gastown prior to transferring to the Vancouver Airport. It's an adventure in elegance from start to finish."

By now we were on cloud nine. As I said good-bye to Marsha, I received a call from Nancy and Lyle Sheets, our Caribbean cruise buddies who are as dear to us as our own brothers and sisters. "We would love to go," they said when we told them about the trip. "Just last week we decided it was time to get away." We began planning our talent night pantomime of "Elvira," originally performed by the Oak Ridge Quartet.

We considered the fact that rather than using a credit card as we normally do with travel arrangements, we must issue a check made out to Marsha Denman, who informed us that she uses checks because of her group and personal discounts. We sent full payment.

We discussed our plans with another couple who also questioned the small amount of money required. I spent several hours verifying Marsha's authenticity. Friends who live near Marsha failed in an attempt to locate the address Marsha had given us. We decided to stop payment on the checks.

The next day our investigators contacted friends who knew Marsha and her father. "We located the house and visited Marsha. The family has lived in the same Michigan community for decades and have strong church ties. We were so impressed with her pleasant personality and convincing story of obtaining fabulous travel discounts and passing it on to others that we purchased four tickets," they said. They also learned that Marsha was on a medical leave with a terminal illness.

Our life seemed to be on a roller coaster. One day we believed in Marsha, the next day brought doubt. "I think everything will be all right," I assured our group. With renewed faith and remorseful feelings that we had falsely accused Marsha, we sent her a Christmas card and another check. Our cruise buddies sent checks also.

The next week, Mel chatted with our mail lady as he opened an envelope. "Here's an acknowledgment for the Alaskan inside passage cruise, but there's no confirmation number. Hope everything's okay," he said. She offered congratulations as she drove away to her next stop.

Mel's Monday morning visit to the mailbox usually discloses junk mail, but the next Monday he opened another letter from Marsha that read:

> Beginning June 1995, visit three islands, Oahu, Maui, and Hawaii; three nights each island for a total of $1,300 or seven nights for $998 per person. Price includes round trip air fare, hotel, transfers to hotel, and car rental on outer islands.

We were tempted to take advantage of this offer, but decided to wait and see how the Alaska plans progressed.

The next page made the following offer:

> California Getaway, Beginning May 1995; seven days, six nights for $250 per person. Price includes a one-day pass to Disney Land, round-trip air fare, hotel and mid-size car rental.

A hand-written note read: SORRY, SOLD OUT. We would have considered visiting my brother George and his wife, who live in sunny California, where retirement desires overpowered his construction business. Rather than vacationing in Alaska, they became engrossed in creating their long-awaited dream home.

The next week, correspondence from Marsha gave us something else to dream about. It read:

EXPLORE EUROPE WITHOUT
EXPLOITING YOUR BANK ACCOUNT!
(Belgium, England, Holland, Germany and France) in fifteen days; for only $1450 per person, (regularly $2725). This price is based on double occupancy and includes: Transatlantic flight to and from Detroit; host service while in Europe; first class hotels, 12 continental or buffet breakfasts, 7 three-course dinners; motor coach; admission charges into sights and all hotel taxes. Trip may be taken between August 1995 and August 1996. If you would like to be a group leader, gather people to attend and a credit of $50 will be added to your account for each person who goes on this excellent European Tour!

During the next few weeks, Marsha called three times to say, "I have ten more openings if you'd like to invite more friends to help celebrate your anniversary." After investigation, self-assurance, with due diligence and in good faith, we made others aware of the fabulous vacation plans. Each time ten more made reservations.

~ CHAPTER TWO ~

AWAKENINGS

Our hopes were dashed when Marsha called to say we would have to change the cruise date. We were suspicious when she stated, "The cruise line is holding three dates for you to choose from. You will receive information soon." This wasn't the only unsettling thing about the situation. A member of our group removed the professional-looking black sticker from the travel brochure he received from Marsha. It was from Travel Agents International in Flint. He contacted this firm and surmised we were caught up in a scam.

Three days later, clutched in our mail lady's outstretched hand was a pre-approved, $15,000 limit Premier Express Gold Card, which we threw away, several department store ads and a large envelope from Marsha. "Priority Mail today," she announced. The wide smile attested to the mounting personal interest. They chatted while Mel gave the envelope a spirited opening.

"This is a long one, three pages," he said. "Let's see what we have here."

"I'll have to hear about it later. You know the mail must go through," she said thrusting the Chevy into drive.

The first page read:

> *Please note the urgent information on the following pages if you are currently registered for the inside passage cruise scheduled for July 16 to 23, 1994.*

The following information made Mel regret his trip to the mailbox:

I have been informed that the Inside Passage Cruise booked for July 16 to 23 has been overbooked and we are asked to move our cruise dates because of the situation. I fully understand your disappointment. The cruise is still scheduled with the Princess Cruise Lines. We have been offered a cabin upgrade, at no additional charge, for your inconvenience should you decide to go with one of the dates they are holding for us.

My heartfelt apologies for any inconvenience this will cause you and your family, but as others who have traveled using my personal discount can tell you, these things do happen but are always compensated in other ways.

Some of you need to understand that the pricing was made available by utilizing my personal and group discount. The cruise initially started out with a small group who have used my discount for other trips, then others indicated an interest to join them. In order to do this, I agreed to field all telephone calls and mailings. The travel agency will hold spaces that I request.

All correspondence, including cancellation requests and questions, come through me. All information will be sent to you, but may not be right on schedule. I handle all of this in my spare time; my family comes first. This may be inconvenient for some, and if that is the case, you are more than welcome to a full refund upon request.

You will find that if going through a travel agency directly, they will charge you the full price amount, not discounted price you are now allowed.

I appreciate your patience with me. The group total at this point is 480.

I have been informed that the alternate date that you choose has been strictly reserved for our group, and will not be overbooked again. My personal written confirmation, and other information will follow by June 1, 1994.

Please note in your records that I will be out of town from April 30th through May 15th. If you have any questions during that time, drop me a line. I apologize for your inconvenience. Thank you for your cooperation.

"What a rude awakening," I yelled. "She sends a letter like this, then conveniently heads out of town. And while she's on vacation, she says she will answer our questions. What a way to ruin my day," I sputtered as I slammed the letter on the table.

Mel attempted to offer solace, "Well, we'll just have to wait and see," he said calmly.

But optimism was high again when we were notified that our alternate date would be held. Marsha issued a refund to our friends who couldn't go on the alternate date.

Our renewed skepticism prompted a verification call to the cruise line who revealed they knew nothing about Marsha Denman or Network Discount Travel. They had no reservations for any member of our group. The largest group scheduled for that date was 130 people from another agency. Marsha would never reveal any data about cruise contacts. She always maintained that the corporate discount number was confidential.

When I was seven years old, my sister Wilma and her husband Herb kidnapped me from a hurtful home situation (another story, that began upon Mother's death) and became twenty-three-year old lovable parents to me. Ten days prior to sailing date, they arrived from Florida planning to join us on the flight to Vancouver. With

18

many years and many miles separating us, these were to be special moments together. We had spent weeks convincing Herb that he would enjoy his first airplane experience.

Marsha called the day they arrived and said, "I have a terminal illness and will be unable to be reached by phone for a week or so. I'm sorry to inform you, but the agent that was handling the accounts failed to turn the money over to the cruise lines and they will not honor the discount. The cruise is canceled and Princess Cruise Lines will issue a refund within eight weeks."

I tried to come up with an easy way to break the news. I found none. Wilma would have created beautiful Alaskan landscapes. Her art classes brought out a hidden capability that surprised even her. Herb and I always laughed and joked, but during this visit he was unusually quiet. Due to their disappointment, they spent only three days in Michigan. I was deeply saddened as I waved good-bye and watched them drive away.

Our cherished plan seemed so sane and practical. Our hopes failed. We were helpless to do anything about it. The emotional and psychological stress that I felt caused an ongoing depression, both day and night. My dignity suffered and self-esteem reached an all-time low, especially when someone made the statement, "I decided to go because I believed in you." I reached the place where I didn't want to face the thirty-four friends and relatives we had invited, or answer the telephone, fearing that the caller would be a distraught person involved in the scam. These people trusted our word that Marsha passed her discount to others in Christian love. When you trust someone's recommendation that a person is honest and true and realize you're involved in a scam, the end result is devastating.

Ailene, my youngest sister, has an extreme love for beauty. I can imagine her exclamation, "Look at those magnificent mountains." She and I love to sing. We had planned a harmonious duet for talent night. Her husband Arnold, recently retired from the telephone company, had planned to take many stunning photos. This would have been one of our few vacations together. When their friends Velva and Ken from Pennsylvania realized they were involved in a scam, their attorney demanded a refund. They received a cashier's check within five days. Others who sent angry letters received checks by certified mail.

My family unit vacation would have been completed with my sister Yvonne and her husband Jerry. Whenever they visited family members, they took along samplings of perennials—starters for their flower garden. Beauty was produced from Jerry's green thumb. Shortly after the trip was canceled, Yvonne had an eye removed due to a malignant tumor. Within a few months, the monster took over the brain; she succumbed to its power. She loved viewing the intricate design of purpling blue mountains, and would have composed scenic poetry while visiting Alaska. Someday, when my Alaskan cruise dream is fulfilled, my memory of her will accompany the view.

Mel's sister Reva, a recent widow, anticipated that a family vacation would aid the grieving process. She and a friend Carol were elated about their first cruise. A group of their church friends booked the same itinerary through an Ohio agency. They declined the invitation to go, saying they were going at a much better rate. "My brother made a thorough investigation. He knows a good deal when he sees one," Reva told them.

When the friends returned from the trip they said, "You're going to love it. It's wonderful." Reva and Carol were embarrassed to say the trip had been canceled. They didn't want to believe that Marsha took the money and cheated people who trusted her. They felt violated.

Mel's sister Evon and her husband Dave, a commercial artist and cartoonist from Virginia, have always wanted to see Alaska. Dave would have created on canvas, the picturesque Alaskan scenes.

Mel was terribly displeased that the family vacation didn't materialize. He is a friendly, congenial individual who wanted our family to take advantage of a once-in-a-lifetime price. His usual happy attitude was replaced by a grim and rigid voice exclaiming, "How stupid can we be?" His sleepless nights were spent reading or studying computer programs. He believes that we will go to Alaska someday, but it will not involve all of our favorite people on the same ship.

Glen and Lillian Siefken have traveled extensively in the United States and foreign countries. They had given us Marsha's number and the cruise information for Alaska, their favorite travel location. Each time we met, we had become more excited about the trip.

I recall the balmy afternoon when Glen, Mel and I sat in our yard discussing our disappointment that the cruise had been canceled. (They had also invested in the European trip.) I had never seen Glen upset. As we talked, he frequently shifted sitting positions and shuffled his feet. His face flushed at times. He was more displeased with Marsha Denman than with the monetary loss.

Two weeks later, total grief and disbelief engulfed us when we were notified that Glen had suffered a fatal heart attack. For the funeral service, the family asked me to express my thoughts of Glen in song. How do you offer tribute and consolation when this stressful cancellation may have contributed to our friend's death?

Owning a business demanded firm travel plans. As a result of the cruise date changes, Glen and Lillian had not taken a vacation that summer. She is now left alone in her sorrow as she attempts to handle an unfamiliar and complicated business.

Rev. Jim and Ann Collins and her brother and sister from Illinois had planned the cruise for Jim's eightieth birthday present. Unforgettable memories would have been made. They may never recover the monetary loss.

21

On September 17, we sent a registered letter to Marsha stating that we were promised a refund within eight weeks and it was now past that date; that we had called and left messages, written letters with no reply and that we expected a refund soon. Her signature indicated receipt of the letter, but again she ignored our request. Most members of our group made a compassionate decision to avoid a lawsuit that they feared could hasten an early death due to her (alleged) terminal illness. Our attorney mailed a letter on behalf of our group. Only one couple received a refund.

It appears that Marsha was goaded with challenging thoughts and desires, and her intense focus on short-term pleasure brought gratification and self-fulfillment.

She spent $600 for an Amtrak club car to whisk her away to The Windy City of Chicago to celebrate the New Year. Subpoenaed bank records show $4,500 in spending money for her $10,000 celebration. That's half of her income, for one trip. There are lots of reasons to head to Chicago: wonderful museums, lively night life, Miracle Mile Shopping Center, distinctive restaurants. The cavernous, glass-enclosed Crate and Barrel on Michigan Avenue. She had reserved a luxurious penthouse hotel suite. She rented a Cadillac, enjoyed elegant dining, compliments of our anniversary party guests. And at the same time, some of her victims on fixed incomes carefully thought about replacement windows and vinyl siding before winter invaded the Great Lakes state.

I have been called a romantic and a dreamer. Another desire, and someday it will happen, is a trip to Toronto to view the stage play, *Phantom of the Opera*. Marsha used our anniversary party guests' money and I'm sure enjoyed those expensive center aisle seats. When my vocal coach Monte Long mentioned seeing the play I said, "I wonder if I could enjoy seeing the production, knowing how much each minute costs." He replied that you feel you're in another world, with the wonderful music, lighting and theater.

In 1994, Marsha bought her second car, traded in the first one. She added up how much money she had, looked at what the pay-off was for the new car, went to the credit union and obtained a loan, to the penny, for what she needed, except she miscalculated how much money she had in the account. She withdrew her money, got the loan and bought the car. When the credit union saw that she was overdrawn by one cent, they advised her that unless she kept a minimum balance of $5.00, the account would be closed. That same day, she made a deposit of $5.01, so in the late summer of 1994, she had $5.00 in her account, when she should have had hundreds of thousands of dollars awaiting final payment for the Alaskan cruise.

Marsha echoed the family togetherness idea. On many occasions, her telephone rang four times, the answering machine clicked on. The recorded voice said: ". . . I will not answer my telephone any Thursday through Monday in order to spend time with my family." (Did she mean to say, *extravagant vacations* with her family?) Many of us dream about treating our children and grandchildren to a vacation such as Marsha gave her family several times. Many of the victims remember the words: "Sorry, Brad and I can't answer your call right now." (We wondered who Brad was.) She concluded telephone conversations with, "Thank you for your prayers."

~ CHAPTER THREE ~

DEAR CHRISTIAN FRIEND

Despite the changes over the years, the spirit of Christmas greeting cards today is much the same as the first commercially printed one in 1843. Early in December, after we sent Marsha a Christmas card and our payment for the Alaska cruise, we received a reply:

> *Season's Greetings to Mel and Pat,*
> *Hope you enjoyed your Christmas holiday. Thanks for*
> *your beautiful Christmas card. Brad and I enjoyed it.*
> *Have a wondrous and blessed New Year.*
> *Marsha*

Thomas Jefferson, our third president and one of the principle framers of the Constitution, called honesty "the first chapter in the book of wisdom." Marsha sounded so honest, so convincing, that intelligent, educated people were fooled. She took advantage of the public's good nature. Her correspondence and stickers on the envelopes read: *Dear Christian Friend, Sealed With a Prayer, Praise the Lord.*

A page of my journal reads: On May 3, 1994, we received another letter:

> *Dear Mel and Pat:*
> *Regarding your 35th anniversary party, this con-*
> *firms your alternate cruise date of July 31 to August 7*
> *on the Golden Princess. Please notify me in writing of*

any trip extension you wish to take, along with any other changes.

Sorry to have to notify you of the change, but it was out of my hands. I will make sure you get a listing of those going within your group when I return from my trip around May 17th. I attempted to call you a couple of times prior to the letter going out, but the line was busy.

Things have really been hectic here, and I am looking forward to leaving town for a bit. Some folks do not realize that I am only doing this on a voluntary basis, to allow others to use my discount along with the group discount.

You folks have been one of the few roses among many thorns. God bless you both and thanks for understanding!

Marsha

When the following letter arrived, our mail lady commented that she disliked delivering information to the cruise victims on her route when it resulted in more disappointment.

July 10, 1994

Dear Christian Friends:

It is with a heavy heart I write to you today concerning the trip you purchased, using my personal discount.

Although I utilized one particular travel agency prior to this cruise, after many problems I had to switch to another. As of today, it was discovered that the reservations were not made by the prior travel agency in a timely manner, and therefore, the discount could not be completely honored. Since the cruise lines would desire an additional amount, double of what you paid per person, the reservations for each cruise, with the exception of the September cruise had to be canceled. I felt it was not right to collect more money from you to hold this cruise, when many expressed how delighted they were to obtain the trip at the rate they did.

I'm sure if you have talked with someone that has utilized my discount for other trips, this has never happened before, and I am sorry it happened for this particular trip. Not only were you planning on taking this eventful vacation, most of you for well over one year, but I have spent much in time, effort and money, also.

After talking once again with the cruise lines, it has been decided that the entire amount each person paid, will be refunded to you within 6-8 weeks. This is an exception to their rule, as they keep a large portion of it usually when the cruise date is so close. The money will be forwarded to me, and upon my receipt, I will immediately forward it to each person that paid. Please know that I am in the process of dealing with the prior travel agency, but will keep a close monitor on each refund. There is no problem in obtaining the refund amounts, as I have received approval and a confirmation number as of this morning directly from the cruise lines.

Once again, thanks for each of you for your notes, cards and prayers sent on my behalf since I have been ill. Although many of us have not had the privilege of meeting in person, many of you have expressed your love and concerns in different ways, and at times when I seemed to need it most!

From what I've been told, this is going to be a lengthy illness, but with the Lord's help, I'm sure it will be a blessing in disguise. Someone was kind enough to pass along the poem listed on the reverse side of this letter and I thought perhaps I'd share it with each of you.

I am so sorry to have to share this news with you today, as we were all looking forward to the trip. May God richly bless each one of you throughout the course of this summer.

Sincerely,

Marsha L. Denman

I stopped reading, broke into a sweat of instant regret. The words, THE CRUISE HAD TO BE CANCELED, caused a bitter taste, like sour lemons, in my dry mouth. My hands felt the coldness of ice water.

Marsha sent cards and letters to victims asking them to pray for her, while she preyed on them. It was difficult to forgive and forget the situation, but I knew I should forgive, because when a stamp on my envelope says, *God is Love* and *Praise the Lord* it means more to me than just empty words. It comes from my heart, not just my head.

Family conflict resulted, husbands and wives against each other, in their belief of Marsha's innocence. Investigation revealed that Marsha's parents attend church, but Marsha went only occasionally. The regular pastor left after the scam became known in the area. The interim pastor attended court proceedings. Some of the victims, because of church ties, would not follow through with a civil suit.

Our next contact with this "Dear Christian Friend" was face-to-face in the Jackson District Court.

~ *CHAPTER FOUR* ~

THE CHAIN OF TRUST

Esther Maddox, a Spring Arbor College teacher, was invited to her former student's home on Easter, 1993. She talked about that spring day, when the delicious dinner and conversation lead to a unique chain of events. Family members told her that they had planned an Alaskan Cruise, a vacation of a lifetime.

A short time later her friends said, "Esther, you must go with us on that cruise. You could never go for less. You can cancel and receive a full refund up to two weeks before departure."

Esther said, "My sister Ellen needs lung surgery and three other family members have health problems. I have made arrangements for a substitute teacher to forward students' assignments to me in Colorado while I care for my family. I'm not sure I can go, although a vacation enjoying God's creations is a valid expenditure and a welcome thought."

Indeed, family turmoil didn't curb the idea to join friends on the cruise. Esther expressed her desire in a letter to her Spring Arbor neighbor. Acting independently and without Esther's knowledge, the neighbor sent Esther's payment to Marsha.

The next week, Esther sent checks for two sisters and five other couples. Marsha thought there was an overpayment and returned the check for Esther's sister Lillie, whose last name is the same as the neighbor who forwarded Esther's payment. The chain of trust became stronger.

Adversity in Esther's life seemed to be without end. While in Mexico visiting Joe, her ill brother, Esther learned that her best friend's husband passed away. She returned to Michigan. Her sister had lung surgery. Her brother Carl passed away.

Esther called Marsha who answered many questions to her satisfaction. Her brother-in-law rounded up ten interested people. She mailed his check for the five couples along with a check for her sister Lillie. They barely met the deadline of May 30. (Marsha called me in June to say she had extended the deadline, and asked if we wanted to invite ten more people.)

A short time remained until the exciting day. Esther's head was in a whirl as she prepared to meet with the Colorado group enroute to Vancouver. "Why haven't we received details?" they questioned. A talk with Marsha always brought a satisfying answer.

June came with many unanswered calls, letters and faxes to Marsha, and no word from Princess Cruise Lines. The chain of trust was strong in the beginning, but had developed a weak link. The day before notification of a date and cruise ship change, Esther wrote Marsha and requested a refund. She received no reply.

She wondered how she was so gullible, paying for two trips, Alaska and Europe, and regretted influencing others to become involved. She was surprisingly calm about her monetary loss, but she felt that worry wouldn't return the investment.

Esther questioned the facts: Can she place blame on her hurried schedule and a year of family and friends' sickness and death? Was it true generosity to pay for her two sisters, and take a loss? Was greed involved? Did the victims fall into the contemporary mind-set of something for nothing, the lotto syndrome, or the pay-little, gain-big gamble? Were the victims just eager for a bargain?

The events surrounding the cancellation of the cruise has resulted in helpful insight regarding trust. The networking chain failed at the source, where the coordinator's family trust resulted in a $22,000 investment. Esther's friend trusted and paid for Esther, because she was out of town. The money was re-paid all along the chain until it reached the source, the link that did not hold.

Helene and Robert DeMain, who live in Davison, Michigan, a conservative community with a strong group of churches, were drawn into the scam through Marsha's Free Methodist Church friends. The retirees said, "We invested $3,400 for Alaska and Hawaii. It didn't deplete our bank account, but it put a big dent into it. Another family invested $7,000 for three trips offered by Marsha.

"We invited three couples who became involved, hired attorneys and received refunds right away. Marsha's mother called and promised refunds. We chose not to pursue a lawsuit.

"Two of the couples that we drew into this scheme were non-Christians. This was an especially bad situation, because it put a black mark on Christians as a whole. Outsiders looked at them and said, 'What foolish people to be drawn in. You can't trust anybody.' The fact that she was a Christian meant absolutely nothing, but Marsha will face a much higher Judge than us."

I attempted to convey my regrets that the chain of trust began with Mel and me and resulted in displeasure for Hal Logan and his family. The children invested over $10,000 to give their parents a special anniversary trip while they were still in good health. It would have been the first airplane trip and sailing experience for the retired minister and his wife. Hal sipped a cup of hot coffee. "Each morning, I wake up realizing we're one day closer to our anniversary cruise," he said to his wife of sixty years.

"It seems that's all you live for," she warmly replied. That *was* all he lived for, until he received the news that the cruise had been canceled.

Talking about the trip gave Hal keen pleasure. His soft brown eyes glowed, his voice wavered and disclosed disbelief at the discouraging news. He felt concern, but no animosity toward Marsha. To add to the family's disappointment, after a lengthy hospitalization, the glow in Hal's eyes dimmed. The family learned that his heart functioned at a 50 percent level and would endure only three to six months. Hal and June's dream will never come true.

Betrayed trust is not only painful, but it creates disappointment and despondence. Trust is always risky. I would rather lose money than my ability to trust. Tennyson's poem, "In Memoriam," states, *. . . I feel it when I sorrow most, 'Tis better to have loved and lost than never to have loved at all.* I believe it is better to have trusted and lost, than never to have trusted at all.

Perhaps we should have risked our money in a different way, by issuing random kindness or senseless acts of beauty. I remember being in the supermarket checkout lane at the end of a very tiring work day. It was obvious that the birth of our son was near. A gentleman behind me said, "Let me help you." As he placed the items from the cart to the counter, I realized that his random act of kindness made me feel like royalty for a moment.

Among the many random acts of kindness my husband provides is to keep the gasoline tank in my car filled. Once when he was out of town, I had to stop at the pump. I was dressed for a business appointment, and the man in the next lane must have had ESP when he said, "My wife doesn't like this chore when she's all dressed up, and I'll bet you don't either. Let me do that for you." I thanked him that I could go to the meeting with a pleasant perfume, rather than emitting a gasoline odor.

Our daughter Leisa brought a friend home one evening. As we sat at the kitchen table and talked, the friend cried while stating a desperate need for a small loan. Mel handed her the money, knowing he would never be paid. Random kindness.

How many times have we thought: These needy people may not use the money carefully. My money may be averted to a lesser cause. The needy may buy cigarettes instead of carrots with my money. Will the money go to the designated charity?

They say a chain is as strong as its weakest link. My English teacher formed a strong link in my life by enforcing memorization. I trembled when she announced that next week's assignment was to memorize "The Rime of the Ancient Mariner" by Coleridge. It didn't matter to me that the water was everywhere, and sailors had not a drop to drink. (With his crossbow, the unfortunate sailor shot the albatross. The defunct bird was hung around his neck and all sorts of trouble ensued.) An albatross around one's neck is an awful curse.

I believe it was a weak link and a classic bait-and-hook scheme to entice vacationers into the travel scam, but Marsha L. Denman found state police on the other end of the fishing line.

The *Jackson Citizen Patriot* newspaper on October 6, 1994, confirmed:

> "Marsha L. Denman, 38, was expected to be arraigned today in Jackson County District Court after a two-month state police investigation of her activities. She faces up to 10 years in prison if she is convicted of the false-pretenses charge and five years in prison if she is convicted of the larceny charge.
>
> When Denman was arrested at her Davison condo Wednesday, October 5, she had a computer running which appeared to contain information about the travel scheme. Kirk Tabbey, Senior Assistant Jackson County Prosecutor, said the State Police Computer Crime Task Force will analyze the material which could result in an additional computer fraud charge.
>
> A $25,000 bond was set on charges of two felony counts, money under false pretenses over $100 and larceny by conversion. Denman, who was led into court with her hands shackled, said she would seek her own attorney."

The Jackson County Courthouse stands on the corner of South Jackson and Wesley Streets. The interior is lined and overlaid with mahogany and marble. An elevator faces the entrance of the marble building. The third floor houses the circuit court, and for the past three years has served as the second home of Senior Assistant Prosecutor, Kirk Tabbey, head of the White Collar Crime Unit and attorney for the Michigan Computer Crime Task Force. Tabbey has been a prosecutor in criminal court for 12 years. He spends many hours on each fraud case, and finds the work fascinating. In his unit they have callous humor, a method of getting around sheer trauma as they deal with every crime imaginable.

Tabbey has sincere deep blue eyes, fair complexion and a well-trimmed beard. He is well educated, honest and adept at his job. He displays a steady, never flamboyant personality. A prosecutor's job is to administer justice. Sometimes he gets close.

So at the age of thirty-nine, Mr. Tabbey took the helm of a ship that didn't sail, and attempted to mend the shattered dreams of 573 people. The wheels of justice started to grind, a beginning in the Marsha Denman story.

CHAPTER FIVE

THE ARREST

A daughter is a lovely blessing to have. Whether she's two or ten or thirty, a daughter is like wearing a personal adornment, a living flower or a piece of shining gold jewelry.

When people pay compliments to my daughter, they're mine too, for a daughter is a special tribute and a projection of mother. A daughter's smile eases the pangs of fatherhood. After all, life's story is written in pain as well as love.

Tabbey first met Shirley and Larry Denman the day the search warrant was issued, when Marsha asked if she could call her parents. They were amazed, upset and kept mentioning that this was a big mistake. They were concerned about their daughter's welfare and Tabbey was too.

At the time of the arrest, Marsha denied that she was working at home, but Tabbey subsequently discovered she had applied for a Home Occupancy Permit to be able to conduct business at her home.

I talked with Detective Sgt. Mark Siegel about the arrest. "We walked across the front porch of her two-story dwelling, rang the door bell. There was no answer. While I waited, another officer went to the back door. When Marsha finally answered the door, after ten minutes, I saw the person who had been a thorn in my side. I gave my identity and said I had a search warrant and that she was under a Two-Count felony arrest. She said there had been 'a terrible mistake. I didn't do anything wrong.' She had a terror-stricken face.

"Once inside, we began the search. On the right was a staircase, on the left, the living room. We walked straight ahead into the kitchen, turned left into the dining room. An upstairs hallway led to Brad's room where I noticed an iguana. Several boxes contained a collection of comic books from the 50s. Marsha's room was next to Brad's. Each room had a balcony overlooking the yard. A retired judge lives next door.

"Marsha said she had given all information to her attorney, but we found computer-generated documents in a hall closet under the stairway which led to the basement where we found her computer. From her condo, we seized several boxes of records from file cabinets, desk, floor and window sill," Siegel said.

Those documents told the story of how she charged travelers a small fee then augmented the total price to make up the difference, thus building confidence that the networking was authentic. The police searched Marsha's car, five credit unions, banks and Travel Agents International.

Sgt. Siegel explained, "I granted her request to take medication, Zestril and Biaxin, that she claimed she needed for lupus and multiple sclerosis. There was no indication of other problems. [A pharmacologist stated that the medication Zestril is for blood pressure; Biaxin is an antibiotic.]

"The handcuffs were tight on her large wrists. We left her house at 10 P.M. Enroute to the Jackson County Jail, Marsha volunteered information. [If an officer asks questions, he must first use the Miranda statement.] She casually talked about Bradley, her 'unemployed house guest' but showed no emotion."

About eleven-thirty, the booking officer on duty called a female security officer who conducted a pat-down search. Next, he grasped Marsha's left hand, pushed each finger into the black ink, rolled the imprint onto the three print cards, reached for the right hand with apathetic firmness, completed the task, then handed her a towel. Marsha removed all jewelry, held the booking number below her chin, grimaced at the photographic flash. The picture and number became a permanent file, which will follow her for many years to come. She was placed in a holding tank to be transferred to the female unit. Drunk prisoners regurgitate in hallways and cells as they are held six hours to sober up, far from a rosy-smelling situation desired by most females. The door breathed shut on its pneumatic hinge and the Jackson County Jail became her home for a night. There are fewer places in the world lonelier and emptier than a cell on that first night behind bars.

The courthouse encountered several escapees until a private corridor, a 20-foot passageway from the second floor, tightened security for prisoners entering various courtrooms, a route Marsha could avoid if she played her cards right.

As he put the pieces together Siegel said, "Marsha Denman has no remorse for any victims. She used Christianity as a tool for her despicable crime and the medical condition to prey on the psychological emotions of her victims." Siegel had a way of smiling to himself as he talked, with his lips pressed together slightly upturned at the corners. I believe this indicated an inner satisfaction that he had additional qualifying factors.

What was intriguing about the whole mess was the next day when she was being arraigned, someone went to the bail bondsman in Jackson county, presented $15,000 and placed a lien on her parents' home. The National Bank of Detroit financed the house. The lien was never entered. The day following her arrest she was released on a mere $25,000 bond. Money was available, but we don't know where it came from.

At the arraignment the parents said it was all a big mistake, that the travel agency was to blame for all this, and it would be vindicated in the end. They refused to give the name of any travel agency that was involved. Tabbey informed them he had evidence and that he hoped they were right because he didn't want to improperly charge anyone. He told them to let him know if they had any information that would help the investigation. Perhaps they believed Marsha's story. Or perhaps they were trying to dupe Tabbey who, unbeknownst to the parents, knew that they had received large sums of money from Marsha a year earlier. Tabbey, however, did not yet know if they were a part of the scam or just concerned parents that didn't know what to do.

The next Sunday's front page investigative update ruined my day with out-of-town grandchildren, which usually involves giggles, grins and good times. I tried to forgive and forget, and enjoy our special day, but found the task difficult to accomplish. I was angry and embarrassed to talk about the half million dollars Marsha accepted from professors, teachers, physicians, investment specialists, a retired FBI agent, people from all walks of life. My sentiments were shared with many others involved. I wondered if she felt a prison term would be worth it all.

We left home early on Thursday, December 1, eager to hear what would transpire on the first day of preliminary hearings, in the case of the People of the State of Michigan vs. Marsha L. Denman. Our steps resounded through the long marble corridors. Planning to take the elevator to the second floor District Court, we entered the double doors. But a contractor had pushed the Basement Level button. The door opened and a sign CRIME VICTIM'S UNIT, jumped out at me. The contractor gathered his equipment as my brain gathered an idea—another avenue to pursue. I moved toward the door while suggesting to Mel, "Let's find out about the Victim Rights unit."

The legal secretary, Karen Knutson, greeted us with a friendly, "Good morning," and introduced us to her boss, Kathleen Hurst. That's how we discovered, quite by accident, someone who really cares about victims.

Kathy is a discreet, attractive woman with expressive eyes. Pictures in her office reveal that she enjoys satisfying her intellectual curiosity and gets pleasure from her home and family.

She became coordinator of the Jackson Victim Rights office in 1993. She has the firm belief that when people become victims of a crime they are thrown into a criminal justice system they know nothing about, unfamiliar with what will take place, other than to show up once they have been subpoenaed to court. Often the victims say they feel left out of the process.

Among those involved in the criminal justice process are the judge, the defense attorney and the prosecutor. But no one represented the victim until Senator Van Regenmorter introduced the Crime Victim's Rights Act and it became law in 1985. It accomplishes a voice for the victims and focuses on their rights. Kathy institutes and oversees these functions and programs. With her help, victims learn to sort out what's going on in the case, giving them a place among the key people.

The Victim Rights office mandate is to acclimate these people so they understand their rights, in layman's terms, as they proceed through the criminal matter. The office staff notifies victims of the scheduled court hearings. Victims may request staff members to accompany them when making oral impact statements.

Her office acts within the system when victims have questions, need to consult with the prosecutor or have difficulty securing services necessitated by the crime. If there's a breaking and entering resulting in damage to their home and they don't know what to do, she refers them to their insurance company. If they have no insurance, she puts them in touch with other county agencies that may offer assistance.

The families of murder victims deal with emotionally draining anger. The criminal process is a fog to them. The Victim Rights office furnishes information and attempts to answer their questions.

What a difference there was between the quiet calmness of Kathy's office and the buzzing activity on the second floor. We sat on a long oak bench in the crowded hallway and waited several minutes for court to begin. I looked through the small window in the courtroom and viewed a worker repairing a light fixture.

I scanned the crowd, eager to see if the face matched the happy voice of the woman that spun glorious vacation plans. I wanted to see the hands that typed the salutation: "Dear Christian Friend." The one I thought was Marsha turned out to be Marsha, but she looked nothing like I had pictured her. She was shorter than I imagined, with brown hair, a double chin and a full, drawn face. Her heavy anatomy seemed to portray a person who has life planned, eager to face the world. She waited without speaking to her relatives who sat nearby. Her father, broad-shouldered and tall with silver hair, comforted her with his protective arm.

At eight-thirty, Judge Falahee's office door opened. The warm room was filled with Spring Arbor residents. Those of us who were fortunate enough to obtain a seat felt crushed as more people packed in. The bailiff adjusted the shades. Light streaking through the window produced rays of twinkling dust. After we exchanged brief pleasantries, a pastoral silence filled the room.

Reporters and television personnel hurriedly set up equipment. A microphone was placed at the podium. Cameras were focused on the witness stand, Marsha, whose face was creased with a frown, and the defense attorney sitting next to her. Several boxes of records confiscated from Marsha's computer were placed on a table. Whispers scattered throughout the spectator's section.

Two tables faced the judge. One was occupied by Tabbey and Detective Siegel, the investigator. The People's table was on my right. To the judge's left was a desk occupied by a court clerk, a woman in her forties, searching through papers. Directly in front of the judge, a pleasant, gray-haired woman neatly dressed in a light blue suit, sat near a stenographic machine.

The judge's desk, a massive mahogany, stood on the left near his office. Calm blue eyes lent a curiously boyish look as he sat in a tall leather swivel chair. I pictured him barefoot at an old swimming hole in a rural Michigan community. I guessed that he was a man whose physical appearance hadn't changed much.

A mahogany rail with a swinging gate in the middle separated witnesses, waiting participants, spectators and curious rubbernecks. They dozed, whispered, sighed and shuffled in and out of the heavy double doors.

The bailiff reminded me of the professor in the movie, "Willie Wonka's Chocolate Factory," as his jolly facial expressions and quick steps brought smiles to spectator's faces.

An announcement was made that the spectators were to meet in a separate room with the Victim Rights Coordinator. We were given a sign-in sheet and instructions to indicate if we were a victim or observer. Kirk Tabbey, who heads up the Michigan Computer Crime Task Force, and Siegel gave knowledge that would be brought out in the hearings.

The authoritative and precise judge articulated his voice like a trained vocalist. He knew what he wanted to say, and said it. He announced and completed four short duration cases, and allowed the balance of the day for Marsha's case.

And the story so many people had been waiting to hear began to unfold.

Tabbey's fine suit rippled neatly as he stood and pointed out to the court that in the two preliminary matters, even though many who were involved in trips were in attendance, he felt it unnecessary that all victims be called to participate in the hearing. He announced that individuals who remained in the courtroom would not be called as witnesses. A list of the people choosing to stay was made available to the judge.

Two charges were named in the complaint. Tabbey enlightened Marsha's attorney that after the search was conducted in October and the charges brought on the same day, additional evidence developed that prompted adding a count of computer fraud, charges of false pretenses using the computer.

The Defense Attorney, Willard Rappleye, gave the appearance of a roarer and a fighter, a lawyer from the old school. His short, stocky build equaled the booming bass voice. Thick gray hair coordinated heavy eyebrows. He asked that the witnesses be sequestered, that the court should advise witnesses they're not supposed to go out in the hallway and tell another prospective witness what questions were asked. Tabbey concurred, and requested that Siegel, his officer in charge, "remain at counsel table."

The judge agreed, and said that victims are in contempt of court if they talk to those on the witness stand. He asked Mrs. Hurst if she made a list of all the people that were there. She answered, from the observers' section, that she did, and gave the list to Judge Falahee.

Tabbey stated that volumes of evidence would be moved as quickly as possible. He gave the defense attorney a black notebook containing new data, and called his first witness, Carole France.

The court clerk said, "I need you to come up here, ma'am. I need you to raise your right hand. Do you solemnly swear to affirm that the testimony and information that you'll give the court concerning this matter will be the truth, the whole truth and nothing but the truth?" The witness said she did. She was advised to "please be seated right here." The unwavering witness took a seat.

Carole France and her friend Cathy Henry were the first to blow the whistle on the travel scam. The community was shocked when the *Jackson Citizen Patriot* headlines, DREAM TRIPS GO POOF, glared at the reader from the front page. A picture showed the two sitting at a table covered with enticing brochures that created several vacation plan options.

The witness stated that she was employed at Jackson Community College and managed the Jackson Recreational Trailer Park. The judge intently watched the witness and Marsha, who appeared to be calm and comfortable in her surroundings, although she wore a fixed frown. The courtroom was silent except for the voices of the witness and the prosecutor standing in front of her.

"How do you know of this person named Marsha Denman?"

"I was contacted by my employer and told that there was a trip going to—" Rappleye loudly objected. The witness continued, "Alaska." Rappleye said he objected to the hearsay.

Judge Falahee said, "Hold on a second, ma'am."

The witness adhered to her purpose on the stand which was to answer the questions. She continued, "And—"

The judge interrupted, "Hold on ma'am, there's an objection. Once there's an objection, you have to stop your testimony." Her face flushed, she appeared to be uncomfortable, nervous. The direct examination had an awkward start.

Ms. France gathered her composure, sat tall in the chair, looked at the judge, smiled and calmly said, "I'm sorry, okay."

She informed the court that on April 6, she sent a $725 check for the Alaska trip, which Marsha signed and cashed. Tabbey asked if she received other information. She stated that due to a diabetic condition she requested special food, and because she has edema, she needed an aisle seat close to the front of the plane. She received a travel brochure for Princess Cruise Lines, a letter from Marsha saying that other travelers have disabilities and she was sorry, but she could not upgrade airline transportation because of the two discounts allowed.

Ms. France said she received letters regarding cancellation, alternate dates and a letter giving Marsha's new address. On July 1, she wrote Marsha saying that the toll-free number had been disconnected; gave her business address for Marsha to mail tickets.

She received no response from that letter. She wrote again on July 15 to confirm the new cruise date, July 31 to August 7.

Tabbey asked if she received a refund, and if she ever went on a trip to Alaska through Marsha Denman. The witness answered each question, "No, I did not."

Marsha bowed her head. A tight fist covered her mouth. After a few seconds she held her head high, as if gaining composure, and looked straight ahead. The defense attorney searched through the witness' folder for what seemed to be a long time. His extensive cross-examination involved Siegel's investigation. Several questions related to whether he came to Ms. France's office, and who initiate the calls. She said, "I contacted Siegel around August 18, by phone, never met him until today in the court room when I saw his identification."

Rappleye went into detail regarding when Marsha promised a refund. At one point she volunteered additional information. He responded, "Would you just answer the question, ma'am."

It appeared from Rappleye's line of questioning, and reference to the infamous "Dear Christian Friends" letter, that he intended to place the refund responsibility on Princess Cruise Lines. Ms. France sent a letter dated July 15, saying she couldn't change her vacation to the date offered. Please issue a refund. She sent another letter on August 7, "My friend and I want a refund as soon as possible. Reply at my work fax number."

At this point, Marsha gulped and swallowed like a kid caught raiding a cookie jar. She wrote on the note pad and gave it to her attorney.

Rappleye finished cross-examination, sat down, stood again and showed the witness a document. In an attempt to establish if Marsha made it known that she wasn't a travel agent, he asked, "It came to your attention July 15, or thereafter. Correct?"

"This letter doesn't even say that," she replied. "Unless it's way down here at the bottom, I didn't finish the last line."

"Read that, those first two lines."

She caught her breath. "Just a moment here."

"To yourself," he demanded. She said the letter stated Marsha was not a travel agent.

The witness glanced at Marsha during Rappleye's inquisition, which mostly included verification of Tabbey's questions. Rappleye sat down as he said, "Cross-examination finished, Your Honor." Tabbey had nothing further. Rappleye lifted his head, slowly straightened up in the chair. Like a fighter staggering to his feet, he approached the witness, showed her a document and said, "Did you understand that Ms. Denman had authored that material about the ins and outs of the cruise?"

Ms. France replied, "I don't understand your question."

"Did you have any judgment that she had made that material up, and printed it and sent it to you?"

"The envelope was all from her. It wasn't from a travel agency."

"I'm not asking you about the envelope, ma'am, I'm asking you, did you have a judgment when you got that material that part of the media that you got was composed, and she caused it to be printed and hashed out in that form? Did you believe it was from some other area?"

Tabbey objected, "It's a compound question. If counsel could just ask it more directly." Rappleye smugly stated that he thought it was a clear question. The court agreed, but rephrased the question for Mr. Rappleye, and asked if that's what he meant. Rappleye said it was correct. The witness immediately answered that she assumed someone else had put the travel booklet together. Siegel searched through boxes for three minutes and found a travel brochure.

At 11:42, the witness was excused and the prosecution called Catherine Henry to the stand. She had a pleasing smile and light auburn hair. She spoke with a dignified clarity and promised to tell the truth. Tabbey's direct examination began by establishing that the witness had never met or talked with Marsha, and that her friend Carole France had arranged the Alaska trip.

Tabbey asked a compound question. Rappleye took advantage and objected for the same reasons Tabbey used with the previous witness. Tabbey warmly smiled, took a cleaning breath and spoke in a calm unhurried manner. "I'll break it down for counsel." The audience chuckled.

Ms. Henry told Tabbey that her check to Marsha had been signed and cashed. He verified the cancellation dates and discussed correspondence received and sent. She searched through the file and stated, "This document, dated July 22, 1994, is where I called Princess Cruise Lines and talked to Kimberly."

Rappleye interrupted Tabbey's method of questioning. "Judge, this is all hearsay and I'm going to object to it." Tabbey argued that he had asked about an admissible cruise line document that spoke for itself. Rappleye continued the objection, "Judge, it's—it's nothing more than hearsay. And it's a statement made by someone else in writing. . . . Pure hearsay." The judge agreed that it was hearsay, stated that representatives from the cruise lines would be called as witnesses, and could testify to the content.

Marsha's head rested in her hand. She looked bored with it all. She removed her glasses, rubbed her eyes.

The witness searched through an envelope and quoted portions of the "Dear Christian Friends" letter. A victim behind me said, "I remember that poem Marsha sent. It says, 'I would rather gather roses without thorns, but I must pluck the thorns though they'll pierce my heart and sting my soul.' It mentioned choosing to share the crown of thorns the Lord wore."

Ms. Henry said her last correspondence from Marsha, dated September 19, 1994, talked about the refund. Marsha seemed to be completely shaken out of her comfort zone. She breathed deeply, shrugged her shoulders, squirmed in the seat, sustained an unrelenting frown.

The prosecutor stated that he had no further questions. He picked up the witness' envelope and sorted through it; talked with Marsha who sometimes affirmatively shook her head, adjusted her glasses again and wrote notes to her attorney.

Cross-examination by the defense concluded after fourteen minutes. The judge excused the witness, requested counsel to approach the bench. Court recessed at twelve-thirty.

After the lunch break Tabbey announced that due to a heavy court schedule there would be no more witnesses that afternoon. Judge Falahee said that ten to thirteen more witnesses had been subpoenaed. "I would like to have everybody here by eight-thirty on January 6, and the entire day will be devoted to this case." He looked at Marsha and said, "Ms. Denman, you're still on bond, and you've turned yourself in, so I'll continue that bond." Marsha didn't reply. Court adjourned; the noises of the departing audience clattered in the corridor.

~ CHAPTER SIX ~

ALL RISE

My husband says I'm an angel—always up in the air and harping about something. As we drove to the courthouse on Friday, January 6, 1995, for the second day of preliminary hearings, my thoughts were in a minor key, harping about our dilemma. I wondered if Marsha and her parents slept or did they lie awake watching the clock? Did Marsha develop additional fears each time a new hour clicked by?

Winter had flaunted her power with icy roads, a temperature of zero, four inches of overnight snow and more predicted, creating a Michigan winter wonderland. As we rounded a curve, the headlights disclosed a line of monstrous oaks and maples. Bundles of wind-blown corn husks scurried across the road. Mel dimmed the headlights, slowed down. My unpleasant meditations were abruptly interrupted by several deer standing in the middle of King Road. We stopped. Their friendly brown eyes stared at us for a while then disappeared into the woods. A black squirrel scampered across the snow-covered roadway.

I had mixed emotions about that morning's happenings. I asked myself, how would I feel if one of my children had been in Marsha's position. My love for them would demand that I support the troubled son or daughter. How far would I go if I felt that child was innocent? Would I abandon my loved one if found guilty?

The bridge Marsha built could require a costly toll for her to cross. The family support that presented itself a few years ago when Marsha's teenage brother died in a drowning accident was again necessary. At Marsha's request, Mrs. Denman called me and several other victims and promised that family members would assist in refunding all the money. She asked us not to sue her daughter.

Marsha sat in silence while waiting for court to begin. She wore very little make up, a red jacket with black trim, a long black skirt and black high heel shoes. Color analysis suggests that red creates an aggressive attitude, while black produces a business-like feeling for an individual. Her family and friends came in full support. A 22-year-old ruddy complexioned male with curly hair accompanied them. He appeared to be free from emotion, expressionless. This was Brad to whom Marsha referred on her answering machine.

Every available seat was taken and the overflow audience stood raggedly along the rear wall. Kirk Tabbey, who had recently received a promotion to Chief Trial Attorney, and Kathy Hurst entered the room. Marsha placed a legal pad and pen on the table, smiled slightly as her attorney pulled out a chair next to him and waited for her to be seated. The bailiff announced, "Please stand as court proceeding begins."

Marsha's attorney left the room. She took several tissues and a breathing apparatus from her purse. Her father left his seat in the observer's section and talked with Marsha. He gave the appearance of being the family leader. He left, and Marsha's sister Lori, who appeared to be an aggressive individual, continued the conversation. She was small built, and looked a few years younger than Marsha. Their mother was heavily built, both legs extremely swollen. She leaned, squeezing a cane as she walked. Her husband assisted.

Siegel and a witness entered the room.

Tabbey announced that the witnesses were in the waiting area and had been sequestered. The judge affirmed that if courtroom observers desire to testify, they must leave the room, that he would break at eleven, resume at one, and if necessary continue another day.

One of the spectators took a seat directly opposite Marsha, fixed a gaze of persistence, as though she planned to paint her portrait from memory. She impatiently tapped her fingers on the seat as the prosecution summoned the first witness.

Mr. Dean Boss was called to the stand. He unwound his considerable height, swore to tell the truth and sat facing the crowded and hushed courtroom. He had a determined look on his sincere, somewhat flushed face.

Marsha wrote on a legal pad while Tabbey questioned whether Boss knew Marsha personally. The witness gave details of owning a business for twenty-two years, heard of Marsha through Woody Voller, who forwarded Boss's check to Marsha and made a reservation for Boss and his wife to take the Alaska cruise.

Tabbey asked the witness what information he had received from Marsha. "Brochures on Alaska sent by priority mail. A fax dated February 15, 1993, about making final payment. It says congratulations on joining others on the inside passage cruise through Corporate Discount Services. The cruise is July 1994, a great experience. Call if you have any questions. Signed, Marsha L. Denman.

"A fax dated April 26, 1994, to confirm Northwest Airlines. A June 13, 1994, fax talks about alleviating rumors regarding the cruise date change. On June 14, 1994, I received the itinerary. I sent a letter to Marsha saying thanks for working with us on the cruise, and about an extended stay in Vancouver.

"On June 19, 1994, I sent a letter saying some friends have not received confirmation, would you please respond to them. On June 20, she gave the closing date for changes. I wrote to ask if Princess

Cruise Lines had our money. I listed names of people wanting to go along. On July 14, 1994, I sent a letter and said I was disappointed that the trip was canceled.

"When I received the 'Dear Christian Friends' letter I sent a reply saying I would like to go in July or August 1995, and that I expected a reply."

Tabbey entered Boss' material concerning the trip as Peoples Exhibit One. Marsha continued writing notes to her attorney. She blinked frequently. Her face became very red. Her attorney looked like he was asleep, but finally moved.

Tabbey knew the answer, but with a concerned look he sighed and asked, "Did you go to Alaska?

"No."

"Did you request a refund?"

The witness immediately responded, "Yes, by phone, letters and her answering machine."

"Did you receive a refund?"

"No."

"Have you scheduled any other trips with Marsha?"

"No."

"Did you tell any friends about the trip?"

"Yes, one friend had thirty-five people in his group. I felt bad."

Thus ended Tabbey's questions.

Rappleye cross-examined: "Have you taken any other cruise?"

"Yes, San Juan."

"How much did it cost?"

"It was free through my business."

"Do you realize the cost?"

"Three to four thousand dollars."

"This Alaska cruise offered through Voller included air and everything, for one week on the boat?"

"Yes."

"Did you believe it was a good price?"

The witness appeared to be offended by the question. "Absolutely," he snapped. "That's why I took it."

The remark brought a ripple of laughter in the observer's section. I heard someone say, "Way to go, Dean."

The defense attorney asked, "Were you booked on that cruise?"

"I assume so. Wouldn't you assume so? I received confirmation."

Attorney Rappleye's antagonism was beginning to show. "I don't know," he said.

The witness made a quick comeback as he questioned the defense attorney. "If you were in my shoes wouldn't you assume so?"

Rappleye looked at his watch, shrugged his shoulders. He asked the witness, "Who informed you that the trip was canceled?" Boss told him Marsha did. Rappleye returned to his seat as he announced, "That's all I have."

Judge Falahee confirmed with the witness that checks were mailed directly to Marsha. He verified that the July 1994 cruise date was changed to August 1994, and later canceled. The witness said Marsha did not respond to a 1995 or 1996 date change.

The judge stood for a few minutes, arms crossed, looked at documents on his desk. He stared into the courtroom as though he was in deep thought.

Tabbey asked the witness to identify Exhibit Three as checks received from the bank. The witness said he had given copies to Sgt. Mark Siegel.

Judge Falahee asked Attorney Rappleye if he had any questions.

"Uh-huh," he replied.

The court reporter, who was busily taking all this down, looked up as if to request a yes or no answer. The judge smiled slightly and demanded, "Say yes."

Rappleye held up an exhibit and asked if the witness had received it. Boss answered, "Uh-huh," remembered the judge's reprimand to Rappleye, and quickly added, "Yes. It gives the address and cruise date, August 22."

"Does it give you the option of canceling?"

"Yes. The new dates were not convenient for us. I said I wanted to go, but chose not to."

Rappleye sat down. "No further questions," he said.

Large snowflakes began to fall. Marsha frowned at her attorney. Tabbey left the room, returned and announced, "The last witness is coming in, Your Honor."

Rebecca Bell was sworn in. She sat tensely upright, prepared for the onslaught. The witness stated her full name, said she had lived in Genesee County for twenty-four years, worked at the school system and the Free Methodist Church. Tabbey asked her to identify Marsha. She pointed to the defendant, describing the red jacket. She knew Marsha in a casual way, through church contacts.

The television cameraman scanned the room, focused on Marsha as she twisted from side to side in the chair. The judge requested counsel to approach the bench. The court reporter intently listened to a sidebar conversation. We waited. A black spider crawled toward the court reporter's chair, making a quick turn in Marsha's direction. I imagined it crawling up her leg, an enormous red whelp, a scream encircling the courtroom. It soon disappeared from my view.

Tabbey reviewed his notes and asked the witness if she was aware that Marsha was involved in travel. "Yes, two couples in the church were going to Nashville. It sounded like a good deal. They asked if my husband Les and I were interested. We sent $250 each to Marsha. We received the itinerary and what was involved."

"What was involved?"

"American Airlines round trip to Nashville, rental car, six nights at the Embassy Hotel, Graceland Mansion, uh, Opryland tickets, Grand Ole Opry. We received airline tickets."

"Did you receive them through a travel agency?"

"Yes, I don't know who mailed it. It was on travel agency letterhead."

"Did you get a receipt? Did you get anything back?"

"No, I didn't get a receipt. We got $25 when we got home. I think it came from Marsha."

"When did you take the trip?"

"April 1993. I paid for it May 31, 1992." [It was a typical pattern for Marsha to hold the victims' money a year or longer.]

"Prior to that trip, did you receive information on another trip?"

"Yes, from Marsha."

"Did you receive any information from a travel agency?"

"No, only from Marsha."

Tabbey handed the witness an envelope. He explained that it was a notebook he would like to discuss with her. He asked, "What are these for?"

"This receipt is for $250, the first payment for Nashville. The rest of payment is to be paid later. This is a duplicate check. Elwood Voller coordinated a family Alaskan trip. The check was cashed at Federal Employees Credit Union."

"Were there any receipts mailed to you with Marsha's signature?"

"A receipt for 50 percent payment for Alaska. Information about paying in full. Here's the Nashville trip itinerary. This is where we mailed a check to Marsha L. Denman, endorsed by Marsha L. Denman. It paid for a Hawaii trip. Here's confirmation from Marsha for the Alaska cruise—Princess Cruise Lines inside passage. This is a July 31 confirmation and itinerary enclosed."

"Does it say Marsha L. Denman?"

"Yes, it gives information about all family member names. This document is Golden Princess July 31 to August 7 itinerary from Vancouver. This is a July 1994 letter from Marsha saying 'Dear Christian Friend: It is with a heavy heart that I notify you that there's a problem with the travel agency failing to turn over information and the cruise lines needs more money.' She said the cruise is canceled. It has Marsha's signature."

"Is there other information?"

"A July 13 update from Marsha. Princess Cruise Lines will not honor discount for '95 or '96. Marsha is not handling it. The Hawaii trip will be handled by Northwest Airlines. We were planning to go on that trip."

The expressions on some observers' faces mirrored their reactions: The same thing happened to me. They talked softly among themselves, while the prosecutor showed the exhibit to the defense attorney. Marsha sighed, shook her head, clutched a tissue in her hand. Her dispirited face reddened. Her family intently listened to Tabbey's questioning.

"You paid for a Nashville trip and an Alaska cruise in 1992?"

"Yes."

"When did you receive information about Hawaii?"

"We paid for the trips in October '93."

"You paid for three trips?"

The witness looked down as she answered, "Yes."

Several observers said aloud, "Oh, no. Too bad."

"To Hawaii?"

"$985 for the summer of '95, a one-week trip."

"Was it a cruise?"

"No, three islands. There are prices like that available through travel agents."

"Did you go?"

"No."

"Did you talk personally to Marsha after the cruise was canceled?"

"Several conversations. I said I'd help contact people. She didn't ask me to do anything."

"Why did she say it was canceled?"

"Because the travel agency failed to turn over information to the cruise lines and they won't honor the discount."

"Why didn't she accept your help?"

"I don't know."

"Did she offer a refund?"

"She said the Hawaii trip would be refunded in thirty to sixty days. She said the travel agency had frozen the accounts. She didn't say how much was frozen."

The prosecutor and the state police sergeant conversed for a short time. Tabbey continued by asking what Marsha said regarding canceling the Hawaii trip. The witness said Marsha told her all trips that she was working on were canceled, that she had $3,500 invested, and that she knew some people had received refunds. She said she had not talked with Marsha since then. Tabbey had no further questions, "You may cross-examine," he told the defense attorney.

Rappleye stood, casually chatted with the witness, establishing that she had known Marsha for fifteen years, attended the same church and that Marsha had arranged the Nashville trip through a travel agency. The witness said she knew Marsha was not a travel agency, and she was still waiting for the refund Marsha had promised.

Rappleye continued questioning. "When was the Nashville trip?"

"April '93."

"Where was Dr. Voller when you sent the check?"

"Concord. Dr. Voller coordinated the family trip."

"After paying for the Hawaii trip in January, did you expect a refund?"

"Yes."

Rappleye ended his cross-examination by asking if Marsha indicated she was raising money for a refund. The witness answered, "Yes."

Tabbey took over the conversation. "What do you know about raising money for a refund?"

The witness replied, "The family is helping. Marsha's mom said they're getting loans, trying to help as much as they can."

The defense attorney was almost lying down in the chair. Marsha made a distorted face, like a small girl distastefully eating her vegetables. She stared rigidly at the far wall. I longed to peek into her brain.

The shrewd, frank and perceptive judge I had hoped for, questioned the witness, "Are you familiar with Marsha's travel service?"

"Yes, friends of mine used it."

"Is Marsha L. Denman an employee of this agency."

"No."

"Did Marsha collect money as an agent for the people?"

"Yes."

"Did Travel Agents International handle this?"

"Yes."

Tabbey informed the judge that Travel Agents International was a witness. Tabbey still had questions: "Is Marsha a travel agent? Did you ask Marsha what Network Travel meant?" The witness answered no to both inquiries. She said she didn't know if she had seen the name Network Travel connected to Marsha.

Rappleye inquired if Ms. Bell had ever written a check to Network Travel, especially for the Alaska and Hawaii trip. She replied that Marsha wanted the check in her name. Rappleye began a conversation with Marsha, who nodded affirmatively several times.

The prosecution called the next witness, Sheryl Trepus, who teaches elementary computer lab in the Davison Community School system and has lived in Genesee county for twenty years or so. She stated that she had known Becky Bell since she was a little girl. She spoke freely and comfortably, "She's my first cousin."

She pointed and confirmed that Marsha was in court today, wearing a red jacket, black slacks. She said, "Marsha attends the Davison Free Methodist Church with me." Tabbey notified the court clerk to let the record show that Marsha was correctly identified. He asked Ms. Trepus if she knew Marsha was involved in travel. She said, "A friend asked us to go on a trip."

I admired the poise, calmness and charming personality the witness displayed as she answered questions. At the same time I noticed that the investigating officer, Sgt. Siegel, left the room.

Tabbey wanted to know: "What did you do to find out?"

"My husband and I talked about it and a friend gave us information. We corresponded with Marsha. I think we sent a check to her."

"What trip was this?"

"To Nashville. I have a folder for April '93. That trip was $500 a couple."

"Did you receive money back?"

"We signed two more people and got a rebate."

"Did she say she would refund the money?"

At the same moment the witness answered, "Yes," Marsha, with obvious boldness, nodded to the affirmative.

"What was covered?"

"Lodging, car rental, attractions—"

The defense attorney scanned the room. His suit coat swayed as he hurriedly departed. Within a few seconds he sashayed to his seat and interrupted the witness to exclaim, "Excuse me, Judge, I see our officer that's running this case is out in the hallway talking to the witnesses. Now that's certainly against the spirit of the sequestration order that you've entered here." He pointed a short forefinger to the chair previously occupied by the officer. "If he's going to sit at this table, he ought to get in here and sit here during this proceeding. He should be in **that** seat."

Tabbey objected to counsel's attitude. He said Siegel was there to assist, to check on witnesses thus creating a case flow in the courtroom. He pointed out that a witness didn't show up. "He's in the hallway getting information. It's perfectly legitimate. If counsel asked, I would have told him that I asked him [Siegel] to go out and see if the witness is on her way. Here he is now, he's back, it's normal course here," he announced.

Judge Falahee ascertained, "Well, if he's just checking for witnesses, I think it's a different story than prepping people for testimony. Obviously, he shouldn't be in here sitting, listening and then telling other people what to say. I'm assuming he's not out there talking. He knows what he shouldn't do."

Rappleye looked at Tabbey and said harshly, "I wouldn't, the way this investigation has been going."

Several members of Marsha's family gave a hardy, "Amen!"

Tabbey continued Rappleye's confrontation. "Your Honor, if counsel has a bone to pick with—"

Rappleye interrupted, "No, I don't have a bone to pick with him." Tabbey returned to his seat while stating that he didn't think this action was appropriate in court.

Not that he felt a need to defend himself, but officer Siegel gave a half smile and said, "I went to the bathroom and I talked to someone, but not about this case."

It was like sitting in an arena watching a three-ring circus, where you expect a roaring lion or a leaping tiger to appear in the next act. Nancy Sheets, who normally takes things as they come—unaffected by what's happening—grinned at the remark and said, "If you gotta go, you gotta go." Observers sneered, chuckled, shifted sitting positions. The judge glared onlookers into silence and when normalcy resumed, the prosecutor and witness continued the conversation.

"Were there any other trips?"

"To Florida. My husband, son and mom."

"What was the cost?"

"The flight, lodging, car rental and attractions cost $275 per person. That was April, '94."

"Did you get a rebate?"

"No."

"When did you pay for this trip?"

"September '92 and final payment February '93."

"What are these checks for?"

"Trips signed up and taken. We sent seven checks to Marsha, two for Nashville, two for Florida."

"What would that trip cost normally?"

The witness answered that they drive the family car and she didn't know the rental cost. Rappleye objected, saying Tabbey was leading the witness. Tabbey changed his line of questioning, "Have you had any dealing with a travel agency?"

"Some of the trips were, but through Marsha. The letters had agency logo."

"Did you pay for an east coast trip?"

"We received papers with ten or twelve trips and prices, Alaska, Caribbean trips. Hilton Head price was $500 for two of us. We wrote a check for California, $875 for three people, which included flight and lodging for four nights. Dates were unscheduled because we still had time before 1995."

Tabbey asked the witness if she had ever taken an Alaskan trip. This question resulted in jesting among the audience that consisted of many who anticipated going to Alaska. The witness paused a moment, said she went in 1962. His eyes widened, he grinned and questioned, "Did that trip involve Marsha Denman?"

The emphatic negative answer brought laughter in the audience. A slight smile dashed across the face of the witness.

"Who else planned the Alaska trip?"

"Family members paid $20,000 to Marsha Denman."

"What did it include?"

"Eight days, seven nights, overnight in Vancouver and flight."

Marsha's head rested in her hand. She adjusted her glasses and placed her hand over her mouth. Her sister Lori, who sat next to me, loudly cracked her knuckles.

Tabbey showed the witness a receipt for Hilton Head. She said Marsha had used the same format for previous trip information. He held up a picture and asked, "What's this?"

As Ms. Trepus answered, "It's a photo of a lady in a hat," a cameraman heard laughter and scanned the audience. This same photo had appeared in every victim's mailbox. The tension had been building for the last two hours and the incident caused a release, like a breath of fresh air. The judge grinned.

The witness continued discussing the various documents: "It's from Marsha. It announces planned Alaska and a Dominican Republic trip, a change of plans. It says we have to select a different date due to a large over-booking in the group. There's 480 people involved. My mom requested cruise etiquette and side trip information. This is a fax giving July 13 to August 6 as the cruise date."

Marsha stared pensively at the judge, but appeared to see nothing. The prosecutor asked the witness about another letter. She told him it was a schedule of the cruise on the Golden Princess for July 31 to August 7, and a clarification of August 6 or August 7 date. Tabbey questioned another document. The witness said she needed her purse that she left in the audience section. The purse was brought to the stand. She searched through it, removed a letter and continued, "This letter says that the reservations were not made by the travel agency and that the cruise lines is requesting more money. She says she's sorry."

Lori continually cracked her knuckles while writing on a note pad, randomly tossed her medium-length hair as if to regain composure.

Tabbey searched through the file, "What's this?" he asked.

"It's from Marsha. She says she's just passing along this information regarding a connecting European trip. We talked about it and decided not to go. I didn't answer the letter." Tabbey gave the exhibit to the defense attorney.

Tabbey asked the witness if she had spoken in person to Marsha about the trips. She had asked Marsha if she was going to get the money back. Marsha told her she would—eventually. Tabbey asked if Marsha told her anything about when or where the money was. She answered, "No." She said Marsha apologized for the inconvenience.

He asked if Marsha ever explained any reasons other than what was in writing, as to why these trips were canceled. But Marsha's attorney objected, saying Tabbey was suggestive, leading the witness. Tabbey said, "Your Honor, I don't think so. I'm just trying to—I can withdraw the question and ask a series of other questions, if it would please counsel."

The judge asked, "Is that what you wish, Mr. Rappleye?" Rappleye replied that he didn't think leading questions were proper.

Tabbey pushed on. "Did you ever ask her anything about why the trips were canceled?"

"I have to think a minute. I believe—I must—I believe that I did," Ms. Trepus said. "My understanding is a combination of written material and what I had gotten from her verbally. My understanding was that there had been a mix-up in the reservations through the travel agency onto the cruise line . . . and it would be impossible to schedule."

Rappleye cross-examined, verifying that the witness had taught school in the Davison system for twenty-four years and had known Marsha Denman about ten years. He questioned if Marsha made it known that she was not a travel agent. Marsha had issued tickets, through a travel agent, to Florida, also a Dominican Republic mission trip. The witness and her husband had scheduled a trip to Alaska, sent Marsha a check. Rappleye asked Ms. Trepus, "She said she'd pay that back to you, didn't she?"

The witness looked at him as if expecting denial that a refund was due. "Right," she answered.

"You believe her, don't you?"

"I do."

"That's all I have."

For one short minute Tabbey re-directed the examination. "You saw the name Network Travel appear quite frequently. Did you ever ask Marsha what that was in conjunction with that name?"

She answered, "I don't think I ever really asked her about that."

"Did you ever get anything with the name Network Travel on it other than associated with Marsha Denman?"

"No."

Mr. Rappleye's re-cross examination went like this: "Did you talk to anyone about this case before you came here to court today?"

"Yes."

"Have you talked to Trooper Siegel about this case?"

"He called me on the telephone."

"When did he call you?"

"Maybe five weeks ago."

"What did Trooper Siegel tell you about this case?"

Tabbey objected, "Irrelevance."

Rappleye argued, "It's relevant."

"It's hearsay," said Tabbey.

Rappleye challenged, "It's certainly not hearsay evidence. He's the chief investigator in this case."

Judge Falahee intervened, "The way your question is formed, it's asking for hearsay. Obviously, it's an out-of-court statement which would be hearsay. If you're looking for the gist of the conversation, I suspect that would probably be more appropriate."

Rappleye quietly replied, "Okay," and rephrased the question, "What was the gist of your initial conversation with Trooper Siegel?"

The witness thought for a few seconds. "I had predetermined to answer questions. But to listen also. And I probably did more listening than I did answering of questions. Wow. I don't know. The questions that he asked me were in connection with, you know, our money in connection with the trip." She seemed to become a little rattled. She had been on the witness stand for about two hours. "You know, our—our—whether we had gotten our money back or not. I remember him asking me that and some other things. He also mentioned several other things that he had discovered in his investigation."

"Did he make any remarks about Marsha Denman?"

Tabbey objected, "Subjective. Asking the witness to call for a conclusion."

Rappleye said, "She's certainly an intelligent witness, Judge. I think she can give the—what her perception was, at least."

Tabbey objected again. "Asking for a state of mind. Your Honor, I believe this whole line of questioning is going again into the outburst that we saw from counsel regarding his opinion of Trooper Siegel in his investigation. I don't know what the relevance to this is and where it's leading, and we would object."

The judge gave the witness permission to continue. "Sgt. Siegel had a great deal of evidence that this money had been spent, but not all of it, however; and that he felt she was definitely guilty of misuse of the money."

Rappleye continued. "Did you see Sgt. Siegel on television?"

"No, I don't know him."

Judge Falahee asked the witness if she expected a refund in six to eight weeks. At his request, she searched through her file and showed him the letter of July 10, 1994. Rappleye asked if Siegel mentioned Marsha's health. She replied that based upon the medication in possession at her house, Siegel indicated he didn't think Marsha had the diseases she claimed she had.

The witness was excused. Counsel approached the bench. After a sidebar discussion, the judge announced that he had a lengthy witness next, so he would adjourn and start again at one.

~ CHAPTER SEVEN ~

THE PHANTOM

During the adjournment, Morty and Donna, from whom we have purchased spring seedlings at their greenhouse, joined Mel and me for lunch. While enjoying a get-acquainted meal, we learned that when the cruise was canceled, they replaced their disappointment with a vacation in the western states. Traveling unfamiliar territory, Morty became ill and had to have emergency brain surgery necessitated from a fall several months prior. The date of the surgery was the seventh day of the planned Alaskan cruise. They were thankful that they weren't on a cruise ship at the time.

I related to Donna that when the sailing schedule changed, our daughter Leisa said, "You must believe what you teach others, that everything works out for the best. I never felt comfortable with the original date." Leisa has a positive and bright outlook on life. I've never heard her make this statement. Perhaps there was some unforeseen reason we didn't cruise on the Love Boat.

When I came across my cruise vacation packing list a few months later, it renewed the disappointment I felt. Most of us don't know what to do with disappointments. I've talked with several victims who handled their let down in the same way that we did.

On the day we would have left for Vancouver, Nancy, Lyle, Mel and I discovered a campground only one hour from home, and took a much less ambitious vacation. Two previous camping experiences involved thunderstorms, a lake of rainwater, threatening floods and returning home after three days. But during that sunny week, as our friends shared their modern camping facilities, I kept remembering the words in a song, *We are **so** blessed.*

The trip kindled an appetite to vary our normal vacation plans. That summer, with the assistance of our friends Peg and Jerry, we made an itemized list—a task that wouldn't have been necessary if we were going on a cruise. The list included cooking utensils, tarpaulin, poles, recreational equipment, and Nathan, our grandson—preparations for van camping.

This new discovery in our life proved that people go out of their way to be courteous and friendly. Campers live in close proximity, share showers and rest rooms and still remain civilized. They stop and talk, but respect boundaries and realize the need for privacy.

They camp in setups ranging from vans, pup tents and pop-ups to expensive motor homes. But in bathing suits roaming the beaches, or wearing pajamas walking the dog, everyone looks equal.

We adopted the joys of camping in beautiful park settings with plenty of trees, played bingo and strolled at night, guided by a full moon and a flashlight. We stayed up late, a real treat for a seven-year-old, made friends with several families, shared food, new recipes and roasted hot dogs and marshmallows on a roaring campfire. A casual comment about forgetting my broom brought immediate response from our neighbor.

The rising sun and chirping birds awaken campers early. You bump your head on the ceiling television as you crawl out of the cozy van bed into the clear, brisk air for the morning trek to the rest room, hoping the line isn't too long. You greet the new day by walking barefoot across the grassy site and discover the smoothness you stepped on was a marshmallow. You breathe a prayer of thanks that your neighbor keeps her poodle on a leash.

The smell of bacon floats through the morning air. You sip coffee while listening to the loons, chipmunks and squirrels. You undergo total relaxation. The children awake slowly. Moms and small daughters, dads and sons, grasp their towels and plastic bag of necessities, and head for the shower rooms. (You hear the response of children who dislike shampoo.)

After breakfast, groups of kids meet at the clubhouse for crafts and story time. Nathan helped "Grandma Pat" read "The Little Boy Who Loved Family Hugs." His friends were proud to be acquainted with the story's main character and the author.

Wherever I went, to the shopping mall, supermarket, and in the courtroom, I heard tales of woe and disappointment regarding the Alaska trip, not only vocal but visual. Sadness in the heart created obvious physical unhappiness, sad faces and health problems.

But there was a happy ending for the family who sat next to me while waiting for court to begin. A Christmas present for children and grandchildren involved $15,000 for Marsha's Hawaii trip. Family members rearranged time off work, bought new outfits to wear. Children were excited, only to have their hopes vanish. The threat of a lawsuit produced a full refund, a welcome surprise in their Christmas stocking. (They took the trip a year later and had a wonderful time together.)

The courtroom doors opened and we occupied the same seat as in the morning session. The afternoon crowd was smaller than usual. Television cameras were set up, NBC, CBS and ABC.

Marsha and her attorney took their seats. He quickly left the room. Marsha removed the glasses that dominated her face, wiped her eyes as she talked to Lori and Mr. Denman. She became more apprehensive during the lunch break, took a bronchial inhaler and tissue from her purse and placed them on the table.

The prosecuting attorney brought in several boxes of records. It was now 1:15. The judge asked everyone to be seated.

The next witness, Laura Muguerza, was called to the stand. She swore that her testimony would be the truth. She appeared to be outgoing, well-versed, gave exact information as she saw it. She verified the spelling of her name, "Z, as in Zebra." She had well-prepared notes in chronological order.

Tabbey's direct examination was to the point. He knew all the facts of the case. Ms. Muguerza had been a manager at Travel Agency International in Flint, Michigan, overseeing the general operations in the front office, for five years.

She met Marsha L. Denman in March 1993 as a client, when Marsha requested a large volume of Alaska cruise brochures. "Of course, my ears perked up because when you're mentioning numbers, large numbers, that's our business," she said. "So we wanted to help. A consumer just couldn't call up a cruise line and order a large number of brochures. If she wanted brochures, I was going to get them. Normally, when you ask for large numbers of brochures, you go through a travel agency. I can request them through a certain department at a cruise line and get them. One of Marsha's faxes stated that after calling around to many agencies, she received no assistance. I faxed notification to Marsha to stop by my office and pick up the brochures. I had several telephone conversations with Marsha, but most of the communication was by fax."

Tabbey asked the witness to identify Marsha. "She's right there and she's wearing a red blazer with black trim," she said.

In her initial contacts, a professional relationship, Marsha faxed a travel quote request for a trip to Nashville, insinuating that the two were competing with other agencies. Marsha mentioned specific things that she wanted included in the itinerary. Victims received various price quotes regarding this trip. It appeared that the price was based on how she got out of bed feeling that day.

The witness said, "Quite frankly, I didn't spend too much of an effort on it. I got her a quote. Marsha came back and said, 'we'll go ahead, this looks good.' It surprised me, because everything was as she wanted. Normally in dealing with people, they're looking for a good value. Usually everybody has a very small budget that they're working with. I have to keep that in mind. I thought Marsha would come back and say, 'well, we need to scale down and maybe stay at a less expensive hotel,' but it was more like, 'I need this, I need that.' She scheduled seven couples for two trips, staying at the Embassy Suites. The total quote price was $10,783.06 for seven couples, close to $900 per person."

The judge desired accuracy also, asked for a calculator, which the clerk provided, "That would be $770.22 per person," he said.

Ms. Muguerza testified that she had received calls from Marsha for Alaska price quotes. Marsha instructed her, "Do not quote prices for trips, refer them to me." She said in June 1993, Lori Denman's name was on a $1,375 voucher paid by Marsha, for rental of a bus that transported quite a few children to Cedar Point Amusement Park in Ohio.

The witness continued, "July 17 through 23, Marsha scheduled a trip to Orlando for Jeff, [Marsha's brother], Tammy, Joshua and Caleb Denman. They flew first class, which is usually pretty expensive. Not often do I have leisure clients who fly first class, business clients do. They stayed in Disney World. That trip was $5,790.95, paid by a personal check from Marsha.

"The checks cleared the bank until we had a problem with a trip to Chicago in December of that year. It was returned for insufficient funds. Marsha eventually came in with a cashier's check. From that point on, we insisted on cashier's checks. That trip included Marsha, Lori Denman and Brad Younce. It was for a New Year's gala, staying at the Chicago Hilton, first class round trip. A limo picked them up at the train station and took them to the hotel. A rental car was delivered to the hotel. That cost was $5,774.00.

"Marsha arranged a trip to Denver for her parents August 3 through 5, 1993. Just round trip air tickets for that. And I should mention that those were also first class tickets. Normally an excursion fare into Denver costs about $300 or so. These two tickets totaled $1,948."

The Judge leaned forward, smiled at the court reporter, pushed his chair away and stood with arms folded. He patiently watched the witness search through her records to answer Tabbey's questions about the many trips taken by Marsha and family members.

Marsha appeared to be frustrated, disconsolate. She rubbed her forehead, fixed a hand on the side of her face, finally cradled her head in her arms. Brad seemed to be bored with it all. Mrs. Denman's pink face looked strained.

The witness said, "In September 1993, there was a trip to Minneapolis. And that was Marsha and Lori Denman and Brad Younce. This included first class air tickets. They stayed at the Registry Hotel, a very nice hotel located close to the Mall of America. They had a suite and car rental. The total cost of the four-day trip was $5,021, paid by personal check."

She smiled easily, leaned back in the chair, gestured expansively as she spoke. "On May 2 through 10, 1994, they went to Orlando. This was Marsha, Lori Denman, Bradley and Joseph Younce. They stayed in Walt Disney World at the Grand Floridian. They had a car, Disney tickets I think. They drove down."

She had receipts for two Northwest airlines, Detroit to Nashville, for $364. Marsha reserved fifty-five or sixty couples for Alaska on Princess Cruise Lines, through Smile Awhile Tours and a day trip to Graceland in Memphis with Grayline Tours.

Tabbey asked about trips booked to Nairobi, Kenya. The witness said she couldn't remember. She gave price quotes for Nairobi, but did not furnish a ticket. She had a fax dated May 25, which responded to Marsha's price quotes for the Dominican Republic.

There was another Nashville trip May 1 through 7 for several couples. The Voller group of twelve people went to Nashville. (A local travel agent verified a charge of $679 for this trip.) Tabbey asked the witness, "Did you quote a price to Marsha other than $10,000? Did you quote $225 per person?"

Ms. Muguerza laughed as she emphatically answered, "You **couldn't do** that."

Marsha talked with her attorney while he searched through his briefcase. She looked offended, bit her lip and nodded at every word as if this was fine. Her face turned crimson. There was a thud of silence.

Tabbey asked about receipts for other trips. The witness replied, "On May 22 to 29 there was a Nashville trip, Marsha and Lori, first class for $2,262.99."

The witness had receipts for Marsha's trip to Toronto, July 31 to August 7, the day Marsha had promised to meet the large group in Vancouver. The witness testified: "Three people, Marsha, and I don't know who else, went to the Sheraton Hotel, a two-bedroom suite which is very expensive. They rented a car to drive there. The cost was $6,243.44."

Marsha's neck flushed. She wore a desolate frown, looked down at her feet occasionally, folded her arms across her chest. The muscles of her jaw tensed. Snow continued to fall, but I'm sure Marsha wasn't concentrating on the weather at this point.

Tabbey asked about the Alaska Cruise. Ms. Muguerza said, "In 1993, she scheduled a lot of trips. I said, 'Marsha you need to book early. Five months, May through September, is the only time people want to go to Alaska. Marsha, you have to make your reservations now.' She would say, 'I'm still working on Alaska.' April 20, 1994, was the first that we booked and held space. I think close to a hundred cabins. And I mean this was the same summer, so it was very late."

Tabbey grinned and asked the witness what was the cheapest way to travel, above being a stowaway. The audience chuckled. The witness maintained her poise, returned the grin and said, "The least expensive cabin on this ship was $2,249 per person, inside cabin. This receipt shows the largest reservation booked by Marsha, a total of 180 passengers, or ninety cabins on the Golden Princess for July 31."

The cameraman focused on the witness who glanced at Judge Falahee. Marsha's attorney held up a brochure that read, CRUISE SPECIALS TO ALASKA. Observers who had received this announcement looked at each other and laughed.

Tabbey continued, "How did you get Princess Cruise Lines reservation?"

"A $15,000 check was given to me from Marsha. We sent it to Princess Cruise Lines and told them the sailing dates. I didn't receive names, and if we don't have names the cruise lines would cancel. We call Princess Cruise Lines with names and requests. They will answer within twenty-four hours. With a deposit, they will hold reservations for one year. We only had three weeks to book."

Marsha's face remained redder than any nosebleed. She looked unsettled and disturbed. She clutched a pen in her hand; her eyes blinked often. Rappleye seemed to enjoy his chewing gum. The judge scooted down in his chair, but carefully listened.

Tabbey asked if the deadline for reservations was in May. The witness said, "Yes, we told Marsha we need money or they will cancel reservations. I hated to lose the space, so I told her again, 'Marsha, Princess Cruise Lines will cancel tomorrow, June 3, for the first cruise July 24, and the second one July 31. Let me know what you want to do.'

"On June 4, I sent another letter. This is the first letter with names. I faxed this cruise information. to Marsha: 'This is in response to my previous letter. Marsha where is the money?' I received her reply saying, 'I'm trying to get a gal at church who will give you the money.' Marsha was in Orlando at this time. She said Sarah Daws is out west and she has the money and that her daughter is trying to reach her. She said, 'My health is not good and I can only work two days a week. I have lupus and recently found out that I have multiple sclerosis. I appreciate your continued prayers.' She said she would send another fax and copies of cruise data with names."

"Did you ever talk to a Sarah or did anyone else?"

"Nobody did. This letter is from Marsha Denman, June 4, 1994: 'Regarding the inside passage cruise, I understand completely about the cancellation and I'm afraid there was nothing further I could do at this point. We're still unable to contact Sarah. If there are any other cruise lines for July 15, I'll pay for it myself.'

"I found Royal Caribbean lines, and held cabins, and no money was sent by Marsha. Another fax from Marsha dated June 6 referred to her request for more Alaska brochures, and fifty Northwest Hawaii booklets. She was also looking for another Dominican Republic group flying in from her church in July. She said, 'We've still not contacted the gal about the money. My nerves are totally shot about the situation. I'll keep you posted.' She wanted to pick up Nyrobi tickets.

"This is a confirmation from Royal Caribbean, eight people to sail July 24. A fax of June 13 said, 'I will pay for this group so they will be able to go, and talk to Sarah Daws. I understand her daughter is going to fly out to meet her next week.' "

The judge glanced at the audience; looked outside to see that it was still snowing. The witness talked about another letter in her file. "This is from Marsha. It says 'Please return the check from Floyd Wells to me and I'll handle it. If anyone happens to call, please refer them to my number.' When Floyd Wells talked to my boss, Sonya, he asked if he would make a check out to Marsha. She said he should always make it out to an agency."

When Ms. Muguerza read the "Dear Christian Friends" letter, Rappleye said, "Judge, that's not responsive to the questions. Just talking on, not responsive. I don't know how I can be any more specific to that. She's just editorializing, going on and on like Tennyson's brook." Tabbey said he wasn't familiar with Tennyson's brook.

Rappleye interrupted again. Tabbey announced, "We'll move on." The judge agreed. The witness said that on July 15, 1994, she replied to Marsha's 'Dear Christian Friends' letter. She received no response.

"What happened next," she said, "Is the documents came in for the five couples who were booked on the Princess Cruise Lines. We notified Marsha, but before we could release those documents to her—we didn't know what was going on—we needed names and phone numbers of all the people. A few days later Marsha had a written notification that she wanted to cancel all the cruises. Sonya refunded Marsha a check for $8,492.50 on September 28."

Ms. Muguerza stated that the next week Siegel came to the agency and they gladly gave him all the records concerning Marsha Denman.

Marsha rapidly searched through a folder. She appeared to be extremely troubled. During the nine-minute cross-examination, Tabbey objected to the detailed discussion of whether Marsha was a travel agent.

Rising, the defense attorney retrieved information from a nearby box and a briefcase, both of which he'd brought into the room at the start of the session. Out of the briefcase came travel brochures. He searched through the box and stated that there were two hundred pages of exhibits. The judge asked for his response regarding admitting the exhibits into court. He replied in a severe tone, "I'm not consenting, I'm not objecting. I just say it's absolutely impossible to go through those in the time allotted. We'd be here till six o'clock if I—" Tabbey interrupted, pointed out that the originals have been made available to counsel since they were seized last fall.

Marsha's face was as red as her jacket. She looked distressed, nervous. Her attorney whispered in her ear. She gave one of her patented scowled, and a negative nod.

The witness had endured lengthy questioning. Rappleye had a way of thoughtfully pacing the courtroom, which added to her apprehension. He verified rates for Alaska and that travel agents deduct ten percent. At one point he asked, "Are you testifying to my question?" The witness didn't answer. He said, "That's all," and took a seat.

The judge winked, or closed one eye, then folded his hands on the desk. He asked Tabbey, Siegel and the Victim Rights Coordinator, to approach the bench. The court reporter exchanged smiles with Kathy Hurst who glanced at the clock and joined what appeared to be a stimulating conversation.

Tabbey called Beth Voller, received no response then announced, "We'll take a break. Mrs. Voller isn't here. The Princess Cruise Lines representative and Sgt. Siegel will come to the stand today." Although the witness had been subpoenaed, she was not called to the stand again.

During the break, it appeared from her hand gestures that Lori was giving instructions to Marsha and her attorney.

I left the room, went to the ladies' room and, as usual, there was a waiting line. I took the elevator to the next floor, returned a few minutes later as the judge announced, "We will adjourn and resume on Wednesday, February 1, at 8 A.M. Peplinski and Siegel will be called to the stand." He reminded Marsha, "Ms. Denman, I'll continue your bond."

Many questions were answered during the two-day preliminary hearings, but many still remain unanswered. I felt that Kirk Tabbey's sense of drama would throw his best curves at the correct time. He had a road map of his strategy including future potential roadblocks.

While waiting for the next court date, a roadblock was thrown in the life of a dear friend, Harriett Riedel. Time passed slowly that cold January morning, as six friends and relatives gathered in the Critical Care waiting room at St. Joseph Hospital. We chatted, glanced through magazines, but concentrated on the completion of Harriett's exploratory surgery.

After eight hours, we learned that the surgery was successful; the cancer had not spread. I experienced a remarkable feeling of relief, prepared to enter her room with questions regarding her health. The same questions applied to those of us who were caught up in the Alaska cruise scam. Will the recovery be quick and complete? What will be the end result? What scars will remain? Will we bounce back and endeavor to protect ourselves from a recurrence in the future? Why did this happen?

It appears that Harriett's recovery will be complete and quickly accomplished. "She's a trouper and doing well," the physician told her husband Earl and me the next week. Not only was I pleased with the excellent doctor's report, but I was delighted when I stopped in the gift shop. A table covered with a cozy pink and blue blanket displayed colorful teddy bears along with copies of a children's book I wrote. An ample supply had been purchased for a get-well surprise for the pediatrics patients.

On January 21, 1995, we received a letter from our attorney, Paul Beardslee, saying Mrs. Denman called him and maintained that she intended to pay for all the travel packages at some point, but she wouldn't commit to a date. She informed him that the police had all the records and people from all over the United States had requested refunds. She asked for duplicate checks for those in our group. She told him he was not speeding up the process by writing letters. He refused her request to talk to Attorney Rappleye.

The line between disillusionment and disappointment is so fine it's almost invisible. Perhaps it's safe to say that when we are disillusioned, often the fault lies with us. Disillusionment is painful, no matter who caused our illusions to crumble. Those in our group have been deceived, misled, a painful result of our cruise invitation. We will feel somewhat redeemed if they receive a refund.

In January, my niece, Nancy Hein, sent a letter to Mrs. Denman regarding the many attempts to contact Marsha. She included a self-addressed, stamped envelope and blank paper, but received no reply.

~ *CHAPTER EIGHT* ~

THE EVIDENCE

The third day of preliminary hearings on Friday, February 1, began with unusual circumstances—no television cameras and few reporters.

We waited in the hallway. When the bailiff opened the door, Lori shoved her way through the crowd and entered behind our group. Marsha took a seat on the front row between her parents, leaned forward in her seat. She seemed to be in deep thought. Brad sat next to Mr. Denman. Silence and a cold stillness filled the room. Lori yawned. Mr. Denman appeared to be praying, then winked at Mrs. Denman. His hand rested on Marsha's shoulder. Lori yawned several times, cracked her knuckles. *Please don't start that again*, I thought. She rested her hand on her mother's shoulder.

Marsha smiled while moving her lips and staring into space. Her face was a warm apricot color that complemented her emerald-green suit. She wore a white blouse, gold lapel pin, and black one-inch heels.

I heard small talk behind me and the words "refund." Silence. Marsha appeared to be crying—or having an allergic reaction—sniffed several times, searched her purse for a tissue. I sat behind her, wondering if she was allergic to my White Diamonds perfume that I had purchased for the cruise.

Lavonne and Ross from Ohio sat next to me. They invested $7,000 in Europe, Hawaii and Alaska trips. The last payment on their retirement gift trip was due the month following cancellation of the Alaska trip.

At eight o'clock, the defense attorney entered the room, talked to Marsha and her family. I heard him say, "the prosecutor." The attorney and Marsha left the room. Her parents stood and carefully maneuvered to the end of the bench seat, made their way past the defense table and into the judge's chambers.

Fifteen minutes later Judge Falahee came in and announced: "I know you're wondering what's going on. We're negotiating."

While discussing the delay, a lady on my left said, "Here we are, we're all in the same boat."

Lavonne said, "Oh no we're not, the boat didn't sail, remember?"

Scott Davis, a local news reporter appeared on the scene, took his place in the reporter's box and began to write. He seldom took notes, yet reported the happenings in detail.

A noticeable change occurred when Marsha left the room. The audience chatted noisily, laughed occasionally. The Davison church interim pastor and three others took seats in the front row. It seemed as though they knew that nothing would happen until 9:42.

The judge peeked in and announced, "It appears that the case will be settled. The attorneys are still negotiating."

An angry voice from across the room said, "I'll bet she's going to get away with this."

Lori strutted to the judge's desk, walked behind it and opened two windows. Sun rays cast shadows on the wall. She plopped into the bailiff's seat. He approached his desk, "You'd better get out of my seat," he said as though they were old friends. She stood, stepped aside. He sat down and immediately sprang back up. "You can have it now." He smiled as he opened the wooden gate and hurried out of the room.

"Okay," Lori replied as she swiveled the chair around and began talking to the interim pastor and the other front row observers. I overheard her say, "The court called our home and said they would negotiate. I hope this is the end of it."

There was a carefree attitude, a feeling of remission in the air. Marsha's friends made small talk, Lori faced the observers, smiled and laughed often. She reminded me of an actress with a captured audience. Brad's face became extremely red as he and Lori chatted.

Across the aisle an observer diligently worked on a crossword puzzle. He appeared to live in a world of words, a world consisting of extinct birds, three-toed sloths, a Greek love goddess and narrow sea inlets. He fell asleep several times, and awoke when his pencil dropped to the floor.

After a lengthy time, the group returned. Although Marsha's lips were tight and firm, she managed a smile for Brad, the second one I had witnessed. The defense attorney shuffled through papers on his desk. The court reporter came in, followed by Siegel, who placed a box on the desk and removed some records. The judge sorted through an envelope.

The bailiff proclaimed, "Please stand for court proceeding to begin—The People vs. Marsha L. Denman."

Kirk Tabbey had a prosecuting attorney's wardrobe of white shirt and distinctive navy blue suit, which hung handsomely on his tall, medium-built frame. His choice of tie today was a bright red silk paisley. "We will resume. Call the next witness, Sgt. Peplinski," he said.

At ten o'clock, Detective Sgt. Robert Peplinski identified himself to the court as a 25-year employee of the Michigan State Police, Southeast Criminal Investigation Division out of Livonia, Michigan. In support of his qualifications, he added that his normal duties were criminal and computer investigations, that in 1990 there was a need between the Federal and State Government to form a cooperative task force for criminal investigation involving computers, particularly fraud. A Michigan Computer Crime Task Force was formed that year, comprised of a representative from the United States Secret Service, Peplinski, and Tabbey, who represented the prosecution's side of it. His job entailed search warrants, seizing and analyzing evidence. He received training through the Michigan State Police and Michigan State University.

In August 1993, he was sent to the Federal Law Enforcement Training Center in Georgia, studying Criminal Investigations in an Automated Environment, a course which Tabbey taught. The training emphasized how computers are used in crime, how to go about seizing them, how to look into the computers and gather evidence, without damaging the computers and data. Once inside the computer he can analyze whether or not it may be hidden, erased, destroyed, where it can be brought back to the forefront. Using a program called HD Century that disallows anyone from writing to the hard drive, he can analyze what is on the computer, copy onto a floppy, bring back erased files onto the drive itself.

Tabbey asked, "How do you bring back an erased file?"

"I use Norton Utilities and sometimes DOS and PC Tools. Norton has a program called Unerase. PC Tools has Undelete, DOS has Undelete. All you do is log onto the hard drive, undelete all erased files. What it does, it will bring up a file that has been erased. By being erased, it's actually still there, it's just that there's a marker that doesn't pinpoint where that file is located. When you give them a marker or a letter or number, it will automatically bring back that file so you can look at it."

"If I have deleted a file with the delete command how do you get that back?"

"I use the unerase, the undelete command. I insert a number or character at the beginning of the file name. It automatically restores that file to readability."

Tabbey wanted to know if Peplinski had encountered any computer hackers or crackers where they booby trap computers that he was investigating. He pointed out an instance where he assisted the Ann Arbor Police Department investigate a hacker that Tabbey prosecuted for using another individual's credit card to purchase computer equipment. In that investigation he came upon two additional hackers who were not particularly a part of this scheme, but a part of another scheme. All three were involved. Tabbey questioned, "Is that the Nation of Thieves?"

Peplinski said that was correct, that one of the investigations led them to Cranbrook University, a prestigious school in West Bloomfield, Michigan. When he did the computer search, he had three chances. The hard drive, which would destroy all data on the computer, was going to be formatted. He was able to by-pass that particular fix that the individual put in. He rearranged internal commands with a directory DOS command.

Although I found the witness' training to be enlightening, the defense was entitled to object, and did, citing the fact of the relevancy of the testimony. Mr. Rappleye stated, "What happened in some other case over in Bloomfield Hills or some prestigious institution—"

The courtroom was exceedingly silent. Tabbey interrupted, "He is an expert, Your Honor."

His Honor questioned the defense and prosecution, "You're trying to qualify him as an expert?"

Tabbey answered, "Yes, Your Honor."

"Mr. Rappleye, are you willing, based upon the testimony, his experience and training, to have him qualified as an expert?"

"No, I don't know. I don't know what he's talking about."

"All right," said the judge.

Tabbey told the court he was almost finished with the line of questioning. The judge said, "Well, it is a very complicated field. If it's something that you're not willing to stipulate to, obviously, the prosecutor can question as to training experience. And this is a limited area of experience to show that he's got experience in this field." Tabbey stated that the witness was qualified to deal with computer situations.

Judge Falahee pointed out that although obviously it was irrelevant as to the terms of the facts of this case, he allowed the testimony to continue. "It is solely for purpose of qualification, is that correct?"

Tabbey said it was correct, questioned what Peplinski did when he encountered the changed DOS command. The witness said he determined that the particular internal files on Marsha's computer were changed. He extracted the necessary information.

Tabbey questioned the security of information gathered. Peplinski said he had a data computer analysis lab, located in Livonia. There's security measures so people can't get inside the lab, only top level bosses or Peplinski's command structure keys. A glass block window on the back prohibits entry. There's a special lock on the door, with only one way in and out. The electrical connections are protected and zoned only for that particular room, which includes temperature and humidity control.

He told the court that once information was gathered, he viewed and printed, verified that it matched up exactly what was on the computer. He provided three notebooks to the prosecution and the defense, made from the computer that he seized in Davison, Michigan.

Tabbey told the court that Detective Peplinski had testified extensively about his training and experience, that there are few individuals trained in this capacity, and that Peplinski had established himself to be an expert in computer crime investigation. Tabbey said he felt that Peplinski was entitled to render an expert opinion concerning the accuracy and reliability of the computer data that had been printed out.

Rappleye had no response. The judge announced that the witness was qualified to testify as a computer fraud expert. Tabbey requested and obtained permission to approach the witness, questioned certification from the Federal Training Center and entered the marked exhibit, Directory Path Listing, a Directory for C files, Word Perfect, Print Shop Deluxe and a data base program.

Tabbey finally arrived at the question many observers were anxious to hear—the results of Peplinski's investigation. Marsha maintained a mask-like expression. She removed her glasses, polished the smeared lenses and resettled them on her red face.

Peplinski had been called to disassemble Marsha's computer system, seize all related data and take it to the office for analysis. He testified that there was a computer, monitor, Hewlett Packard bubble jet printer, keyboard, software and paper. The computer displayed a letter, possibly to a travel agency. He saved the file, powered the system down, disconnected the system, seized all computer equipment. He gave Siegel a return form on the search.

Peplinski took precautions to insure that the hardware and software would be protected from external destruction or damage. He turned the police radio off to prevent an electronic field circular motion due to transmission, which could destroy data from the hard drive or on floppy discs. He placed the seized equipment in the back of his Chevrolet Blazer, where it would be level and flat and not subject to jarring around from any motion of the vehicle. He took the equipment to his office, placed it securely into the computer lab, locked it up and it remained in that location.

Tabbey verified with the witness that several documents were "identical, exact similarity" to those Marsha sent to the victims.

Peplinski affirmed, "I found a data base management program, dBase, on Marsha's computer, which stored files, summarizing them in a particular order: names, address, locations, in alphabetical order. So you could have all individuals from a particular city, such as Jackson, Michigan, all located in one particular file. And you could see where your letters are going." He also confirmed that she had used and stored the picture of a woman wearing a hat, standing at the rail of a cruise ship. The same picture was identified earlier by witnesses who stated they had received it from Marsha.

When Tabbey moved for admittance of People's Exhibits, the judge asked Mr. Rappleye if he objected. The defense attorney showed Marsha a document containing highlighted information. His cross-examination involved extensive questioning regarding execution of the search warrant, who was present, was there evidence that Marsha had received or taken any money and placed it in accounts that were in names other than her own. Peplinski said he did not. Rappleye questioned if most of the material seemed to be communications to a travel agency in Flint. Peplinski answered that he didn't recall, but it would be a small amount.

The defense attorney appeared to be uncomfortable and frustrated when relating to computer-generated documents. He advanced toward the witness with his short-legged tread and said, "Bear in mind, that I'm basically computer illiterate." He paused squarely in front of the witness and showed him a document. The witness said he wasn't familiar with the file. Rappleye questioned, "Now this computer system could print letters that would not be on the reserve or the—in the—in the system, that wouldn't be, whatever it's termed, [the witness helped him out by saying 'on the hard drive'] on the hard drive."

When asked if Peplinski indicated there were other documents available to be seized, he said he didn't seize any hand-written material. Rappleye said, "That's not the answer—that's not the question. You searched the apartment with a search warrant?" He replied that all he did was seize the computer system and left.

Tabbey and Rappleye discussed a document. Rappleye laid it on the table in front of Marsha. She had the uneasy look of a woman who had left her purse elsewhere, which is also the look of a woman in serious trouble. The judge swiveled his chair, his blue eyes gazed out the window that overlooked the county jail.

The witness was dismissed. The prosecution called Detective Sgt. Mark Siegel, who marched to the stand. He was tall, dark-haired, military-looking in his Michigan State Police uniform. He gave his name and briefly recounted his considerable experience as detective and investigator—seventeen years as Field Training Officer—training new troopers that graduate from recruit schools at the East Lansing State Police Academy.

Siegel was enthusiastic, self-assured, experienced at giving evidence and one of the best in the business. He became involved in the case when he received a telephone call from Carole France on August 23, 1994. The witness had given the court an account of her contacts with Sgt. Siegel. He verified correctness, saying he had collected copies of documents and checks that victims had sent to the Marsha Denman residence and that every day he gets more mail.

Siegel investigated financial institutions, presented information to the prosecutor, requested and obtained six search warrants. He had a two-fold purpose; to collect financial records and to find out if there was money in any accounts. He had orders to freeze and seize them.

He was assisted by law enforcement agencies from the Flint Post. He stated, "When we go into another jurisdiction that has a police department of their own, we notify them that we are there. It promotes good police business among agencies. It's a matter of respect of authority for that jurisdiction." The arrest warrant was for a two-count felony for larceny by conversion, and a felony charge of false pretenses over $100. He served a subpoena on Laura Muguerza at Travel Agents International, General Motors Institute, and the Jackson Credit Bureau for all files relating to Marsha Lee Denman.

Marsha appeared impassive as Tabbey questioned the detective regarding the arrest warrant and search warrant involving her residence and the 1994 Pontiac Bonneville. Siegel stated that when he entered the building, Marsha and Bradley Younce were there. He identified Brad, a white male with brown hair, green slacks, tan shirt and tie, seated in the front row. Tabbey asked the observer, "Is that correct Mr. Younce?" Brad nodded. Tabbey said, "He's nodding yes, Your Honor. May the record reflect that Mr. Younce has been correctly identified."

Marsha's attorney objected: "Judge, I don't see the relevance of it."

"I don't see the relevance either. He's not on trial," the judge quickly replied.

Tabbey said, "No, he is present."

Judge Falahee said it was all right. Rappleye's voice raised several decibels. "Intimidation, I guess is the word for it." The judge ordered them to proceed.

The officer identified Marsha as a defendant in the courtroom and present at the time he went into the building to conduct the search warrant. He said, "I had made an attempt prior to going there, to establish who owned the building. I talked to the Davison Township Officer, Donald Brocke, to attempt to contact the owner of the residence. I was advised that Marsha doesn't own the building. I called the tax office to see who owned it. At this point I was advised that it was a very nice—"

Marsha's attorney objected. Siegel continued, "A building. I understood that it was a condominium-type structure."

Rappleye objected again, "Hearsay, Judge."

Tabbey withdrew the question; said he didn't wish to get into any discussion. Siegel continued, "We were trying to avoid smashing in the door of a nice place with a battering ram or a foot. We tried unsuccessfully, however, to get somebody with a key to go in, based upon the search warrants. We came close to actually kicking in the door because there was no response." Siegel said he was wearing a suit. Trooper Henke and Trooper Juneac were in police uniform. The Davison officer, David Scarabek, had not arrived yet.

Marsha's face reddened, jaws tightened. She shook her head in absolute frustration. She watched the witness between glances at the judge. Brad, who maintained a blank stare, had a blood-red face. Marsha's life took a turn for the worse on October 5, when she finally opened the door. She called her parents and a Flint attorney.

Siegel went on, "I said this is in regard to the Alaska cruise. She said the records were in the hall closet. I found a large amount of records. We searched the closet, the upstairs bedroom. I looked through the Franklin Day Planner for July 1993 and 1994. There were a number of victims I had contacted. There were no checks, no cash, no bank statements. I found passbook savings accounts. It was paper clean, absolutely nothing. I searched all of the ceiling ducts. In the basement, there was a letter on the computer screen, to Byron Wirthingshaw in Canada, a file cabinet with folders, information on car, telephone, income tax and a Europe trip for 1995-1996."

The witness said that the news coverage team from Channel 12 arrived some time before the search was complete. The parents arrived. Siegel spoke with Mr. Denman who was less than enthusiastic. Siegel said, "I informed him that this was a crime scene, I was in control of it, and he was not going to direct me how to do my job. I told him, 'You can go outside and stay there. Or you go to jail. So you're not going to interfere, unless you change your attitude,' which he did. At that point I allowed him to come inside, sit at the dining room table with his spouse. And he was pretty much a gentleman after that."

Tabbey asked, "Did you determine if he was upset for the circumstances that he found his daughter?"

"Sure. I can understand that he was upset. He remained calm throughout the rest of the time."

"Did you take Ms. Denman from her dwelling?"

"Yes. She was taken to Flint. I transported her to Jackson."

"Did you harass her?"

"No, she invoked the Miranda Rights. She called her attorney, Mr. Jerry O'Rourke, with whom I also talked on the phone."

"Have you served a subsequent search warrant?"

"Not yet."

Rappleye's cross-examination began at 11:44 A.M. He asked Siegel to explain how Channel 12 got there when he did. Siegel said they had asked him to contact them, which he did, prior to the search warrant. He was unsure when Ann Nortangelo and her cameraman arrived.

"Did they take pictures of her apartment?"

"I can't say what they did."

"Did you observe her? You're in charge of this crime scene; I assumed you'd be. But you let the TV people walk around at their discretion. You told Mr. Denman he wasn't to walk around, you made him sit down. Correct?"

"That's what I told Mr. Denman, yeah."

"Did they—I think you said they came in the apartment and photographed the interior of the apartment."

The witness seemed agitated. A stern voice displayed that from the start of the investigation, there had been animosity between the investigator and the defendant's family. "I beg to differ with you. I never said that."

"You didn't say that?"

"No sir."

"Did you give an interview to Channel 12 at that time?"

Tabbey objected. "Your Honor, it has no bearing on what's conducted." Rappleye said he thought it had relevance. Tabbey argued probable cause, that a crime was committed and that Marsha Denman committed it. He stated he didn't understand the relevance of an interview.

Rappleye said. "I'll get to the relevance, Judge. I assure you that it's relevant. I just don't want to tip off Tabbey and officer Siegel."

The judge said he would allow the questions, that the purpose of a preliminary examination was for the prosecutor to prove the elements as well as proving probable cause and that the defendant was involved in committing the crime. But it's also for the defendant to discover information and things that may be relevant as far as the case is concerned.

Rappleye whispered to Marsha and continued: "Sir, the question was, didn't you give an interview at that time to Channel 12 and its camera people?"

"I talked to them."

"In front of the cameras, and commented upon the evidence, did you?"

"I don't recall if I did or not."

"And didn't you comment upon evidence that you seized in front of the cameras that day sir?"

"I could have. As I said, if you were listening, I don't recall."

"And didn't you comment upon the probable guilt of Ms. Denman?"

"Not to my knowledge."

"Didn't you comment that she was engaged in a scam involving hundreds of thousands of dollars?"

"Alleged. They asked—they asked me what we were investigating, so I told them."

"And didn't you tell them that you had seized something like $75,000?"

"Possibly."

"That wasn't true, was it?"

"It was $71,900."

"That you seized in this case?"

"Been recovered."

"Recovered?"

"Supposedly that Denman had sent cashier's checks back for refunds. It was, I don't recall, I don't think I could have told them that it was because all these were receipts that were stapled to the forms we found in the closet, the document packets. So I had no way of totaling up the numbers. So I would say at this point, no, I couldn't give them a figure."

"You didn't recover any money that day, did you?"

"I testified to that before."

"Is your answer no or yes?"

"No, I did not recover any American currency that day."

"That's the answer I want, thank you. And didn't you tell the Channel 12 that she was living in a condominium?"

"I could have."

"That wasn't true, was it?"

"It's what I would call a condo."

"It's really just an apartment, isn't it?"

"It's a condo."

"A condo is when the occupant owns—"

Tabbey asked the court if counsel was testifying. Rappleye pushed on, Tabbey objected, "Counsel, Your Honor—"

The judge interrupted, "Hold on a second, there's an objection."

Tabbey again objected, saying, "Counsel has apparently tried to go after the credibility of the officer—" Rappleye agreed, and Tabbey finished his sentence, "Credibility of the trooper by whether something is an apartment or condominium. I don't know that that's relevant. It's certainly a collateral matter and shouldn't be pursued."

Rappleye challenged, "It's putting a different lifestyle in her public image. She lives in an apartment. Rules of conduct state that you can't comment on guilt. Tabbey was on the floor that day."

Tabbey seldom referred to his notes, but efficiently pressed on. He asked and answered questions to the point. "Am I awfully confused, Your Honor? I interviewed no one that day. The trooper was available. This case involves removing evidence and bank records. I have not violated any ethics. Is he going to argue?"

Rappleye attempted to justify Marsha's extravagant lifestyle, "The fact is, she doesn't live in a condominium, she lives in an apartment. And for all of this stuff that she's just wallowing in cash, that's the public's image of her from reading the paper and listening to the television people. I think that's relevant at this point and time. There's also some other considerations, reference to rules of professional conduct and commenting upon evidence that is going to be used in court. And commenting upon the probable guilt of any person charged with a crime. I think it's dog-gone relevant.

"And that goes right to Mr. Tabbey because he was in charge of this investigation and he was on the floor that day. I suspect Tabbey authorized the search warrant. Tabbey was at the so-called crime scene. Yet he says, 'I'm just looking here, observing what's going on.' That is somewhat disingenuous in my judgment. He's the one that called the computer people. He's the one that wants to make a computer case out of this." Rappleye sounded serious, full of energy. "The Flint paper has quoted Tabbey. That's going to be a factor in this case. How can he wash his hands and say he has nothing to do with it?"

Tabbey became more emotional as he spoke. This clever and professional prosecutor's statements were short, rapid and aimed like arrows. "Counsel seems to enjoy making misrepresentations, including that I was fooling around with my hands in my pocket and staring around, which is apparently what counsel likes to do. He wasn't there. He's taking the word of a defendant in this case who was arrested and taken away.

"Apparently the news stations had already broken this story, had interviewed Ms. Denman and subsequently got lots of calls from a lot of areas. It was already out to the general public. Scott Davis here, has been following this case and printing stories and information. I don't know what Mr. Rappleye is getting to, where he's trying to go with this, other than create a smoke screen or to impinge on my credibility. I am not even testifying. What we have here is a situation where a computer was found. The computer was confiscated because the trooper asked the correct authority to do so.

"Trooper Siegel indicated to me he did not have the requisite knowledge to take that down. I called an individual who did. And he came to the scene. I did not search, I did not retrieve evidence. I did not direct them what to do. I don't know what else he's trying to indicate here in trying to impinge that I have any control over these troopers in their job. We let them do their job. We do not interfere with their job. They're there to obtain facts, obtain the evidence, and deal with it in a fashion that they believe is professional and what needs to be done.

"I was there in case they found a link to the money. A seizure warrant was prepared to prevent anyone from going to any bank or location to remove any funds from accounts. I was there in case we needed to prepare any other search warrants for any other banks if we found additional locations where money could be. And, in fact, there was none found. As the court is aware, we found a grand total of a couple hundred dollars in accounts. We intercepted $8,000, and we have indications from our work that there are hundreds of thousands of dollars missing.

"Certainly no one went on the trips. If counsel has problems, he should be talking to his client. He should be talking to the victims in this case who gave interviews well prior to my becoming involved in this case. If he's alleging to pin anything about bad publicity, he should be taking that up with the news media and not our office or the trooper," he concluded.

The judge swung his chair around, cleared his throat. "This has gone beyond a question of condo versus apartment," he said. "We're questioning the trooper's involvement now. Continue."

Rappleye asked if statements were made to the press that Marsha was living in a high style and had an expensive bed. Siegel responded, "I consider a $2,289 bed pretty expensive. I could have." Rappleye asked the judge to strike that answer.

When questioned if Siegel indicated to the press that Marsha was faking her illness, he said, "I had my own opinion. I could have." Siegel discussed the arrest in detail. Tabbey excused him at 12:05 P.M.

The judge asked counsel to approach the bench for a moment. Tabbey asked the judge to bind the defendant over on the charges contained in the warrant and complaint, a charge of three counts.

Rappleye objected, claiming that the third count of computer fraud came late, after all the testimony had been taken, and he didn't see anything very fair about it. "You go to court and you're supposed to know what you're charged with. And after the preliminary examination, all of a sudden, out jumps another ten-year felony.

"The counts are internally inconsistent. And if you're guilty of the five-year count, you'd be guilty of the ten-year count or vice versa. I don't think that we should be bound over on all counts. I object to the ten-year computer count. I can't say I'm surprised, but I think the proper way is to charge it and then try to prove it.

"My client couldn't be found guilty on all counts. There is no doubt in this case that several people have been reimbursed. To say it's fraudulently taken is absolutely off the wall. Your Honor, I would ask that you dismiss this. **There is no evidence that anyone has been defrauded in this case!**" Rappleye picked up his file folder and sat down.

The entire courtroom moaned a collective sigh as though Rappleye had punctured a balloon. They scowled at each other. The baffled spectators shuffled their feet on the tile floor, mumbled and displayed objection. The family in the front row seemed to be unmoved.

Tabbey gave a clear, concise rebuttal. "In 1992 she started collecting funds for a cruise. She accepted checks made out only to her. The cruise dates were in 1994-1995. She said it was all set for 1994. She claimed to be Network Travel, which existed only in her mind and on the papers that she produced. When she did book, she paid cash just to get them booked. There was $8,492.50 held—the refund from the cruise lines.

"As stated in the computer fraud statute, she used a computer to store and retrieve information. In accessing computer, she used resources to create official-looking documents. There are over 300 pages of victims. The time frame in this case is from 1992 to October 1994. She booked additional trips to convince people she was authentic.

"While she was on sick leave from General Motors Institute, a $20,000 a year job, [Rappleye objected to both statements] she paid $32,000 to a travel agency for herself and her family.

"The trips didn't exist. She claimed the delays were based on travel agent's actions, and that is untrue also. She has no money in any of the accounts. These trips couldn't possibly be booked for $725. She committed a larceny act when she converted it over. The false pretenses are she never ever worked with Princess Cruise Lines. She produced documents showing her contacts with Princess, wrong dates, wrong schedules of sailing times, totally inaccurate. All are consistent charges. And we ask that she be bound over on all three to face trial in circuit court."

Marsha bowed her head, appeared to be hopeless, depressed, when her life took another downturn. She shuffled her feet, adjusted sitting positions several times, tossed Rappleye a superficial glance.

The judge addressed some of the technical arguments that had been raised by Rappleye. Testimony showed that the defendant used a computer to commit the crime, justifying the addition of the third count. Judge Falahee was satisfied that the elements of these crimes had been committed and there was probable cause to believe that the defendant was involved. He said there was case law to support the fact, and the issues would be addressed in circuit court.

The judge instructed Marsha, "Ms. Denman, you stay in contact with your attorney about your next court appearance." The exhibits were returned to the prosecutor for safekeeping. Arraignment in circuit court was set for February 28, at 8:30 A.M.

Thus ended a three-day preliminary examination linking Marsha to a scheme for cruises that never existed. Tabbey and Rappleye had clashed over whether authorities unfairly tainted the case by granting media interviews during the highly publicized investigation, and faulting the investigator for portraying Marsha as someone who owned an expensive $2,200 bed and that she lived a high lifestyle.

When court adjourned, a Channel 6 TV representative gathered his equipment and rushed from the room. Marsha and her family followed. The reporter, with a camera on one shoulder and a bag chucked full of equipment on the other, stood near the door. Mr. Denman pushed him aside as he sharply commanded, "Get outta my way." The reporter scrambled to retrieve the camera before it crashed to the floor. The cameraman told me he had arrived after the proceeding began and wasn't allowed to set up the equipment. He appeared to be frustrated and distraught.

Several observers lingered in the hallway. After the cameraman's many interview attempts failed, he scanned Donna and me reading a letter that one of the victims had received a week ago from Marsha. She asked everyone to understand her situation; said she was innocent. (Marsha and all witnesses had been sequestered.) At the same moment, Sgt. Siegel purchased a copy of my latest book. The cameraman focused on my signature while making the statement that the relatives mentioned in this book were involved in the ship that didn't sail. He asked how I felt about the situation. I said, "I'm sorry that so many people trusted others and discovered that Marsha was unreliable, and I regret encouraging others to lose money; however, we must find it in our hearts to forgive, regardless of the outcome." The interview resulted in book sales from local viewers.

The prosecuting attorney summarized the day's happenings to Channel 6. The cameraman thanked us and smiled as he left, realizing he had reclaimed his job status, something to report for the six o'clock news.

Cameras and microphones picked up comments, some enthusiastic. One of the victims exchanged sharp words with a newsman, "I hope this court grants my wish for a maximum punishment. She spent my pension checks having a good time."

An elderly woman slowly extended a skinny finger with white nail polish and pointed it at her companion, "Is this how a rape victim feels," she said. "Like it's your fault, like you should have known better than to let it happen?"

A victim who had invested a large amount of money overheard a conversation, fought back tears and joined in. "If only Marsha could realize that we sacrificed, withdrew money from our savings and borrowed enough to have a family reunion—and it didn't happen."

Donna, Morty, Mel and I amicably relived the day over lunch at Red Lobster. We said good-bye with a question about whether Marsha would waive the formal arraignment in circuit court or would she appear and enter a guilty plea.

Federal authorities are keeping an eye on Marsha Denman as her travel scam case winds its way through the courts. They are proceeding with a dual prosecution that may take years to accomplish. Marsha formed a complex mail network nationwide, which included three continents.

Rumors began to circulate that Marsha was in the Dominican Republic. "Oh, no! That can't be true," I shouted. "She's smart enough to realize she can't leave town. Maybe it's just an April Fool's Day joke."

Spring had awakened. Yellow daffodils emerged from the March snow. The crabapple blossoms near our front door brought a week's delight.

Upon arrival at the 12th District Court on April 21, we were surprised and overwhelmed to discover that neither Marsha nor any family member appeared. At the pretrial conference, the judge and attorneys determine if the parties are ready to proceed, or if the case can be resolved without going to trial. A jury trial date had been scheduled in the event this matter could not be resolved at the final pretrial.

Judge Charles Nelson's courtroom was more spacious and comfortable than Judge Falahee's court. Blue velveteen drapes covered the large windows. The green juror chairs looked more comfortable; the spectator's bench seats were padded. His court was the first in Jackson County to use video cameras. Each courtroom will be video equipped, as the budget permits. The observers whispered, anxiously waited to confirm what we had heard.

Kirk Tabbey and Rappleye took their places. The bailiff announced "All rise," as the chamber door opened and Judge Nelson came swishing out with long purposeful strides. I noticed a unique feature, collar-length, dark but graying hair, parted in the middle and neatly slicked back. He mounted to his place as a rustling apprehension fell over the room.

Marsha's attorney stated that Dr. L. Vallance who specializes in internal medicine, notified him that his patient, Marsha Denman, was being treated for an active condition of lupus and that she was physically unable to be in court. Rappleye maintained that the three counts charged against his client appeared to be overlapping. Without further comment on this statement, the judge remarked that another date was scheduled May 12 at 8:30 A.M., and that perhaps Marsha would be cured and available by then.

The prosecutor disclosed that the investigator, Sgt. Siegel, had been transferred to the Jonesville State Police Post. Court was adjourned at nine.

On Friday, May 12, the courthouse was a beehive of judicial activity. Lawyers, clients and observers roamed its tiled corridors and worked their way to the various courtrooms.

The observers were pleased to know that false rumors had circulated and perhaps Judge Nelson was correct to assume that Marsha was well for the alternate pretrial conference date. "She looks well," I heard an observer's sarcastic opinion.

Marsha wore a beige rayon blouse, black skirt and vest and an agonizing look upon her flushed face. Mr. Denman assisted Mrs. Denman as she made her way into the room. Brad followed behind. At eight-thirty, the bailiff announced, "All rise, the People vs. Marsha Denman."

A Channel 6 TV reporter and *Jackson Citizen Patriot* Newspaper reporter Scott Davis took their places. Judge Nelson announced that everyone should "be seated." He established that he had received a motion for a reprieve. He asked the defense, "Is there anything you need from the prosecution in terms of what they provide?"

Rappleye answered, "No, I'm getting papered to death." He took a legal pad from his briefcase and began to write. Marsha glanced across the room. She sat with her ankles crossed, elbows resting on the arms of her wooden chair.

The judge asked the prosecution, "Is there anything you need from the defense?"

Tabbey homed in on the fact that he had received nothing from the defense. In accordance with the Discovery Rule, the judge asked the defense, "Do you have a list of witnesses that you're going to be calling? Do you have any expert witnesses? Do you have any exhibits to admit to show to the prosecution?"

Rappleye answered "None" to each question. His voice was losing its professional restraint.

At the pretrial conference the court must know, by court order, that both sides are doing what they're supposed to do, sharing the case they both have. For the last ten years, the prosecution in this court system had been having to provide everything they had. There was a "trial by ambush," meaning that the defense prepared nothing and the prosecution had to arrange everything. The defense attorney stated that the prosecution had been researching and had lots of material, but he had no exhibits. The defense offered no challenge, no witnesses, no defense characters, and no evidence. There was no jury waiver at this time.

The day in court was informal and short-lived. When the judge questioned if they were looking at a six-day trial, Tabbey agreed and informed him that he intended to file any final motions at least two weeks prior to the trial. The judge rejected the original court date. He accepted and announced that a jury trial date had been set for July 31.

Mel and I felt an obligation to explain the status to the victims in our group. I sent another letter to Marsha, reminded her that she promised a refund within six to eight weeks, and that I expected her to keep her promise. I received a call from Mrs. Denman who said, "Marsha is not permitted to contact any victims, but she cried when she read your letter. . . . Surprising information will be brought out in the upcoming trial."

The prosecution can ask for a bench trial, where there is no jury, but the judge will make the decision on the case. This would be advantageous to the prosecution. If Marsha doesn't take the stand, the jury as well as the victims will want to know why.

Summarizing his many contacts with the defense counsel by comparing the facts with an open hand of poker, Tabbey said, "I continued to supply the defense counsel with some of the best cards in my hand, knowing who held all the cards in the game Marsha was playing. I watched his expressions as he threw a top card and I threw a better one. I said how are you going to beat that? He answered, 'I don't know.' It was clear at that point that he was resigned to defeat at trial."

Tabbey spent twenty-four hours going through bank records to prepare a chart showing a forensic audit for everyone to see. He could trace the money from one account in which Marsha washed more than $200,000 starting with the Vollers' to the collapse of her enterprise in August 1994.

The defense knew the chart would be prepared in large bold letters. Tabbey told counsel he would prepare another audit chart showing how much money came in to Marsha, what her legitimate income was and where she spent it, including a $13,000 check made directly to her parents—money deposited from the victims' checks. Those dollar amounts would be setting there through the whole trial for the jury to inspect. Rappleye knew this would produce a tremendous impact, and was finally able to convince Marsha of the strength in the case against her, the realization they'd caught her. They had proof and evidence that could no longer be hidden. Her basement scam was unraveling in the light of day.

Tabbey disclosed, "There has been no evidence of criminal activity in the family. No evidence yet uncovered that relatives or friends were directly involved with scheming money from the people. It is evident from the records, that large amounts of money came from the victims and went directly from Marsha to friends and family. I don't know if Marsha's family has properly filed and recorded for their tax records, the money given to them, but clearly they knew what was done and they were involved at some level."

Early in the process of justice for the victims as well as for Marsha, the family—many still believing in Marsha—talked to investigators then they became quiet as they started to see the case mounting. Bank records show checks written in large amounts of money. Maybe they questioned where the money came from. What answer did Marsha give to convince them that this was legitimate? She may have duped her own family and friends into believing that this was money that could be used by them. Yet she constantly told everyone, especially GMI, that she was not earning any money from this. If she was not earning any money, then how could she just hand over money to members of her family? Her attorney mounted a legal challenge and filed a motion hearing maintaining that Counts Two and Three are the same and should be dismissed.

A significant legal ruling that had a negative impact on the prosecution's case was made at the motion hearing on Friday, June 2. Marsha was not required to appear. Her attorney was in the courtroom when Tabbey brought in a large stack of records. I slumped in my chair and stared at the floor, looked at my watch as the minutes ticked away. The hearing finally began at 8:45 A.M.

Judge Nelson's black robe billowed about him as he took his seat. With modest seriousness and dignity he stated that a motion had been entered by Mr. Rappleye concerning the question of charges, basically double jeopardy. "If I turn money over to you and you keep the money it's false pretenses. If I loan you a car and you don't return it, it's larceny. The people gave the money to get a cruise and it didn't happen," he said.

Tabbey agreed, "The larceny by conversion should be dismissed since she intended to steal the money from the start. The cruise didn't happen. The money was paid. The computer was used to accomplish the task."

The judge initiated an open discussion. "From your facts, she used the computer, the telephone and mail for fraud. Charging that the computer bulletin board is used is not the essence of the fraud. It's the telephone that is involved. The computer was an additional role, not the major role. It could have been Xeroxed. It could have been printed."

Tabbey pointed out a similar situation. "The Jemison case is a welfare fraud case. The defendant there used others to become involved to gain access to the computer. Referring to the case of false pretenses, it talks about the purpose of obtaining money. Denman used a device to do this. That case used printouts. She used Princess Cruise Lines logos and compiled numerous lists with that heading. Can you imagine typing thousands of names on a typewriter? With a computer she can do this easily. She didn't involve print shop people. By having access to a computer, she could do this on a large scale. She took from others."

"Did she use a modem? Did she contact the travel agent with a modem?"

"She used a fax. She used the system in her basement and generated this fraud on a large basis. The fraud was perpetrated by the computer and sent through the mail. It was the device that was used in a fraudulent way. We showed in the preliminary hearings that this was the device she used. The form she used was found in every victim's mailbox. She had access to the computer and this is not a situation where she sits at home and plays around with a computer, but she input data and used it to mail hundreds of letters. She couldn't do it without the computer."

"She could have done it with E-Mail or a typewriter."

"It's a two-part section, device and access. The question is she could have done it with a typewriter and had it printed at a higher cost, but she used the computer."

"Many people have a home computer."

"She had file cabinets, desk, everything she needed for a complete office situation. This is more than input/output storage. You could not have eliminated the part of the system of which digital switches are the heart. Using a computer a 12-year-old at home can access TRW [Credit Information Services] and attack 500 files. That's still a home computer, but technically that doesn't leave out the fact that the computer was used. The law says *to compute*. It doesn't say a *home computer*. It's a separate act from a crime regarding a car. The computer handled the printing. She could have hand delivered it, but the computer still created the forms," Tabbey concluded.

The judge asked, "Mr. Rappleye, do you have anything else?"

Rappleye replied, "It's not fraud." The judge ignored the comments of disagreement in the observer's section.

Rappleye waited for order and continued. "In reference to computer fraud, if a computer is accessed in any part of the scheme she could have Count One and Count Two. As to whether the computer statute fits this case, I can't argue that it does. The statute isn't well drawn. The computer made it easier to compile a list. Old typewriters had memory. I'm computer illiterate. I think there's three charges here of the same purpose, the theory of how much do I love you, let me tell the ways. The prosecutor is looking for more ways."

Judge Nelson said, "We've lowered the count to two. It should be invalid to Count Three. There was no retention of ownership of the money. A home computer is like a typewriter. The computer was used in the fraud, also the telephone and mail was used. Count Two stands, Count One is dismissed."

What had occurred regarding charging Marsha with false pretenses over $100 and larceny by conversion over $100, was for every individual that was defrauded, a separate count of a ten-year offense could be brought, which would involve hundreds of counts, and make each one a separate trial in itself. By combining it into one overall scheme, two things could be accomplished: limit the amount of prosecution, and get the maximum benefit of the punishment while allowing the Federal authorities to pursue their investigation without causing any grounds for double jeopardy.

Within a few minutes we filed out of the courtroom. I wondered, *How many times will we enter and leave this building without an end to the Marsha Denman story?*

Part of the answer came on Friday prior to the date of trial, when Tabbey found out that there would be a court date, but not a jury trial.

~ *CHAPTER NINE* ~

THE PLEA

Monday, July 31, 1995, was a crushing day. After toast and coffee, Mel and I headed for the Jackson County courthouse. A heat emergency was in effect, humid and uncomfortable as the Midwest can be in mid-summer. Temperatures continued to range in the 90s, having claimed the death of over 500 people in the Chicago area.

We arrived early, sat on a wooden bench seat in the long hallway, assuming the courtroom was locked. At eight, Kathy Hurst arrived, sat next to me and chatted. When she saw the bailiff, she excused herself and returned a few minutes later. Attorney Rappleye hurried down the hall, chest out, his brown tweed sport coat swaying. Mel opened the door for him and whispered, "Your zipper's down."

"I'll check that out," he said with a grateful smile.

Following close behind him was Kirk Tabbey. Mel opened the door and as Tabbey entered, he said in a hushed tone, "She's ready to plead to the charge." The news media and I entered the court-room at eight-thirty. It's a rarity when court sessions begin early, but we discovered that at twelve minutes after eight, the judge had announced that court was now in session.

Sitting at the desk on my left next to Tabbey was Angela (Mina) Lloyd, the attractive assistant prosecutor Mel had assisted with a large box of records. They had arrived at eight o'clock sharp, with complete audit posters, 4- by 6- feet, big enough for everyone to see. Ms. Lloyd was new on the case, brought in to assist in preparing the audit and other demonstrative evidence. She was medium height, in her late thirties, with shining dark hair, gold jewelry, a businesslike navy blue suit and white blouse. She glanced a friendly smile at the observers as she moved about the courtroom.

Marsha and her attorney were seated to my right. The only family member accompanying her was Mr. Denman, who was casually dressed in a sport shirt, instead of the usual suit and tie. The defense attorney stood and declared that his client entered a plea of no contest.

In the courtroom it was as though Tabbey had a check list, went down it item by item. He exploited everything that Marsha had said. He didn't mince words, but brought straight details and facts according to the prosecutor's documentation and proof, and blew Marsha out of the water as far as credibility goes. She made a big splash, but didn't tread water well.

"Your Honor, we would appreciate a guilty plea. A civil liability is evident. In the summer of 1992 Ms. Denman began to defraud to obtain group cruises at a bogus cost. This fraudulent act has a value of over $100, a felony which carries ten years."

The prosecution was ready for trial. They wanted a guilty plea because they wanted to go to jury trial, so they objected to the no contest plea. The decision to accept a no contest plea doesn't hinge on what the prosecution says, however, it's at the full discretion of the court. It was inevitable that the prosecution would concede that civil liability was a certainty. Marsha waited so long to make the decision that she didn't have a chance to beat the prosecution. The judge accepted civil liability as a valid reason for the plea of no contest and stated, "The specific date is April 6, 1994."

Tabbey replied, "Your Honor, we filed an amended information to reflect the proper time frame for the fraud. The court made

107

the correction. I charged this file as a time period not a specific date. When it was charged by the chief assistant, he put down one date rather than the entire range of time that I had wanted to do."

There was a lack of communication. At the preliminary examination, Tabbey moved the court indicating that he intended to expand the time of the original complaint to reflect the fraud period which was the summer of 1992 through 1994. At the examination, it was changed. In circuit court the records from the court failed to show the time, so the charging document incorrectly showed April 6. The amended information corrected it. The court was reading from the old information.

Ms. Lloyd, Attorney Rappleye and the clerk began searching through a stack of records. Tabbey indicated to the court that there was an amended date to the April 6 information, and that all other counts were the same. The court needed to locate it in order to conduct a plea. The prosecution found a copy and gave it to the court.

The judge asked Rappleye if he had a copy, and how did he plead.

The defense answered, "Yes. We plead no contest."

The courtroom had grown hushed, like pre-dawn solitude. Ruth, the circuit court clerk, asked Marsha to raise her right hand. "Do you solemnly swear that the information that you'll give the court will be the truth, the whole truth and nothing but the truth?"

Marsha quietly answered, "Yes."

A woman with hair cut short above the ears and in the back, and bangs extending to her dark-rimmed glasses, sat across from me. Slouched next to her was a teenage daughter with brown curls that lapped over her thick glasses. Her cheeks and nose were round. Her legs were long and thin. She forgot to comb her hair. This was the second time I'd seen her in the court room. Her attentive seriousness indicated that perhaps someday she would pursue a career in the court room.

She half-whispered, "Mom, what's the difference in telling 'the truth' and 'the whole truth' and 'nothing but the truth'? Why don't they just ask them to promise to be truthful?"

The mother's confident eyes maintained a calm steadiness, "I'd like to hear this, if you don't mind," she said. "We'll talk about it later." *I've wondered about that too, what is the difference in the three,* I thought.

The next day, a visit to the library satisfied my curiosity. The three kinds of truths are stated explicitly. Some people try to avoid promises to tell the truth. To "tell the truth" means that they must not lie in response to the question.

"The whole truth" means something else. For instance, a governor, in another state, proclaimed that he had moved 15,000 people from welfare to work and omitted adding the fact that in his state, 23,000 other people moved from work to welfare at the same time. He told "the truth" but failed to tell "the whole truth." The end result was that 8,000 more people were on welfare, not 15,000 fewer.

Witnesses are asked to tell "nothing but the truth" which is another concept. For example, if a person tells the truth in response to a question and then adds a lie, he or she has told "the truth" but failed to tell "nothing but the truth."

Marsha and her attorney stood at the desk as the judge discussed her plea of no contest. She frequently shifted positions to compensate two-inch heels. She wore a straight black skirt, off-white blouse and a black muted print vest.

Judge Nelson asked, "Do you have any questions regarding these charges? How do you plead?"

The face of the woman about to speak was agitated, but Marsha answered calmly, softly, "No contest." The no contest plea suggests that she knew she was in real trouble with civil liability and possible additional criminal prosecution. That's the throw-in-the-towel, or find-me-guilty-and-sentence-me plea. Her plea up to now was "not guilty" and she changed her plea to "no contest." She cannot automatically appeal. She can only file application as long as she is sentenced. She could get turned down, since there's a new law in Michigan that purges appeals.

Prior to going into court, Marsha told her attorney, and he informed Tabbey that she would have a jury trial. Today's surprise element was when Marsha realized the cards were stacked against her. Tabbey had played his cards right, the defense had folded. Ms. Lloyd positioned the audit chart, which was used previously as evidence, so that it faced the judge. Since Marsha's focal point and attention had to be on the judge, it served as a constant psychological reminder. The judge paused thoughtfully and asked, "Were there any promises or threats to get you to plead this way?"

"No."

The judge asked a series of questions: "Are you represented by Willard Rappleye? Are you satisfied with his representation? Do you understand the charges? Are you aware that you are charged with a felony which carries a ten-year sentence? Do you know that it carries a fine? Do you understand that if this plea is accepted, you will give up a trial by jury? Do you understand that if there's no trial the court presumes you innocent until proven guilty, and that you give up the right to have any witnesses appear in your behalf? Do you understand that the prosecutor has the right to prove beyond a reasonable doubt that you are guilty?"

Marsha's gentle, reserved reply, "Yes," added to the observers' quiet seriousness.

In accordance with Michigan sub-rules, the judge asked the prosecutor and the defendant's lawyer if the court had complied with Michigan Rule 6.302. They answered, "Yes, Your Honor." Marsha seemed unusually calm. Mr. Rappleye stood imminently near.

The judge must determine that all evidence points to the fact that the crime occurred in Jackson county. He asked Marsha, "Did this take place in Jackson County?" She answered that it did. The bailiff shook his head to the affirmative. I wondered if he was also a victim.

Tabbey scooted down in his chair while talking with Ms. Lloyd. There was a long pause while the judge searched through records, reading them carefully. The court reporter patiently waited, occasionally smiled at the bailiff.

Marsha shifted standing positions again, glanced up as a local newspaper reporter took his seat on the right. She had little or no makeup covering her ashen face, a definite change from the crimson look on previous court dates. Her hair looked recently permed. She remained extremely calm. Her attorney's hands were neatly folded behind him.

The judge explained, "I've reviewed the preliminary examination. It indicates that from 1992 to 1994, in Jackson County, the defendant cheated residents for an Alaskan cruise at a cost of $725. The plea of no contest is accepted and entered. For the record, I have made no agreement to sentencing. We don't want the case to be set for sentencing within the usual 30-day time frame since she intends to make full restitution to all remaining victims."

Rappleye interrupted the judge to state that some restitution had been made and will continue to be made prior to the sentencing date. Tabbey said he didn't object to the end of September because he felt Marsha should have thirty days to get the money and make restitution.

Judge Nelson stated, "Sentencing has been set for September 27, at 8:30 A.M. Mr. Rappleye and the defendant will go upstairs to enter an appointment with the probation department."

The probation department must arrange a time to meet with the defendant so they can make a Pre-sentence Investigation Report. They need to know everything about Marsha in order to sentence her. They investigate the family, friends, her boyfriend, her background, prior criminal history, the incident itself, the version that the victims provide, the nature of the offense, how many people were defrauded, what effort, if any, she's taken to remedy the situation, and try to come up with the restitution figure. The probation department scores the severity of the crime which gives the judge an idea of how to sentence. Her payment of restitution to victims would also influence this sentence.

Rappleye moved from the defendant's position to a nearby desk. Marsha followed him, leaned against the chair then sat down. Tabbey, Ms. Hurst and Ms. Lloyd stood in a circle with their heads bent together in busy consultation. The judge looked through documents on his desk, rested his head on his hand and waited for the conference to end.

Marsha and her attorney were instructed to go to the fifth floor. She leaned over the bench and talked to her dad, who was solemn and shallow complexioned. He remained silent, and slowly, deliberately, without touching or looking directly at her, followed Marsha, who moved in a matter-of-fact way. She looked stoic and withdrawn. She appeared to be beaten, as if the taste was sweet initially, but became pungent when her world came crashing to a halt. In my mind, she was relieved that step one was over and the drama in her life was approaching the final act. But the finale was still a mystery.

Ms. Hurst and the prosecutors reconvened as the bailiff looked on with interest.

Tabbey asked, "Your Honor, may I approach the bench?" Siegel, who conducted a full investigation in the case, joined the conversation. Tabbey continued, "If Marsha Denman was serious about returning money to these people we need to know what money was owed and what had been returned. The only way to do that is, with Sgt. Siegel's help, to begin an elaborate contact in our Victim Rights Coordinator's Unit, by going through hundreds of records from victims around the country to create a victim data base by sending out questionnaires. We need a full data base that will be used for Federal authorities in their upcoming prosecution."

They dispersed at eight-thirty. The judge began another case.

When we left the courtroom, Tabbey noticed several victims gathered in the hallway discussing their astonishment at the turn of events, namely, that Marsha never indicated she would ever admit she did anything wrong. He suggested a meeting in the Victim Rights Advocate's office. A dozen or so people crowded into the room and for fifty minutes, many questions were answered.

Tabbey said, "In one bank, $4,700 went to Lori, Brad and Marsha for train and hotel accommodations, $4,500 in travelers checks. Another credit union $20,000 to $30,000 was run through. Due to a computer operator improperly programming the purge command, all the statements past January 1993, checking account and records were accidentally purged. The documents that were on micro-fiche are there, but they don't know how to get them. The bank security tried to locate as much as they could. They were unable to physically look through all 1993 records to give an audit. It is unknown how much money went through that checking account although $200,000 was probable. One deposit at an ATM machine was over $9,000—checks from the Alaskan Cruise. The IRS will verify that.

"If we had gone to trial, I had an audit prepared to display Marsha's account involving another banking institution. We brought enough evidence to fill two days' testimony. I indicated to the judge that we would have the final evidence list to him, 200 to 300 exhibits, by the second day of the trial. We were ready to go when Marsha decided to end it all right there. It was the old adage that if you're not prepared for trial, the trial will go, but if you're ready and loaded for bear, the bear will usually turn itself in."

That evening, as though to confirm what really happened, I rushed to the paper box and picked up the newspaper. I glanced into our neighbor's yard and thought about the leukemia battle

113

Dick lost a few weeks ago. His wife Bernie disposed of their 40-year-old treasures. She put the house up for sale. "Come over and get the canopy swing you've admired for so long," she said. "Dick would like the idea of sharing it with a good neighbor."

A perfectionist's work showed as Mel sanded and painted it white with country blue accents. It sets stately under the spreading honey locust waiting for an occupant who is eager to relax. A nearby table holds my iced tea and chocolate chip cookie treats. Anticipating a cool evening breeze, I made my way to my favorite leisure spot and opened the *Jackson Citizen Patriot*. The headlines shouted:

WOMAN CONVICTED IN TRAVEL SCAM TOLD TO REPAY $200,00. *A Davison Woman convicted in a travel scam fraud has until November 15 to cough up $200,000 in restitution to repay over 500 customers who purchased bogus cruises from her, or Judge Charles A. Nelson will book a trip of his own for Denman—a state prison for at least four years. This morning, Nelson ordered Denman to repay the money as a last-ditch attempt to get the victims some of their money back. Denman has repaid about $100,000 but prosecutors contend she owes $350,000 more in restitution. . . . If she repays $200,000, Nelson said, he will then place her on four years' probation. Failure to comply will result in a sentence of four to 10 years in prison.*

"See Denman, p. A-2" the newspaper said, and I flipped the pages. A title for a caption occurred to me: 'The Foolproof Plan That Failed.' I read on:

It is not clear where Denman will get the money; prosecutors say they believe the money is largely spent. Denman, surrounded by family members, declined to comment as she walked hurriedly from the courtroom.

Pat Lively, a Spring Arbor resident who purchased a bogus Alaskan cruise from Denman said she was hurt that Denman used Christianity to trick fellow members into buying the trips. She has a simple formula for a sentence: one week in jail for every person she defrauded.

Calling her the Jim Bakker of Michigan, Prosecutor Hurst blasted Denman for living an extravagant lifestyle while defrauding fellow church members. "The truth is Marsha Denman is a thief, and one of the worst in Michigan's history," Hurst said.

Siegel was the warrant officer conducting the investigation. Six weeks before the trial date, he received a promotion to another jurisdiction, with other duties to perform under another commanding officer. That left the prosecution to pick up the pieces and do the remaining work to get ready for trial.

Tabbey and Siegel were anxious to continue the investigation. They were determined that if they brought these charges, they would make them stick. They realized this would be a big case.

Marsha's attorney realized at the preliminary examination that the prosecution had a tremendous case against his client. I believe this skilled defense counsel went to all the weaknesses of his defense: What about these personal and corporate discounts? What about the mountain of incriminating documents that the defense received from the prosecutor? Marsha tried to come up with vague explanations, indicating they're wrong, "That's not true," she said. She asked for prayer for her accusers, namely Mr. Tabbey and Detective Siegel.

The documents were the products of Denman's imagination and the latest word-processing and database software in the computer market. These high-tech tools are the instruments of choice for the modern con artist—the fraud artist's magic bag. It can generate any kind of form you want.

Denman's partner in crime, the computer, became a chief witness against her as Michigan State Police located and downloaded her deleted files to build the case against her. Marsha's crime is only the latest example of a rising number of computer crimes in recent years. More and more hackers are breaking into computerized networks, electronically bilking stores and banks.

Bob Crompton, a U.S. Postal Inspector, is investigating this case and gathering information for a Federal Grand Jury Trial. The week of July 31, 1995, Federal court subpoenaed Marsha for handwriting analysis. Tabbey's entire file (four large boxes) was subpoenaed to Federal court. If she is found guilty there, they stack charges. Siegel met with Joe Seitz, Internal Revenue Service investigator. Marsha refused to divulge any details regarding an FBI agency contact.

Ross and Lavonne Love drove the five-hour trip from Ohio, arriving at 8:40 A.M., to find an empty courtroom. They called that afternoon. I explained what happened, made plans for a visit and added, "And that was that."

I sat under the mighty locust tree on August 13, enjoying my yard swing, iced tea and the evening paper. "Scott Davis definitely has a way with words," I told Mel. The *Jackson Citizen Patriot* headlines read:

COMPUTER WAS IN ON WOMAN'S TRAVEL SCAM

The information highway ran smack over Ross Love, and he didn't even know it. Love received confirmations, travel receipts and other documents, bearing decorative logos and the name of the agency was called Network Travel. "They were official looking," said Love, a 67-year-old retired agricultural economist. They could have come from a travel agency." Alas, they didn't.

~ CHAPTER TEN ~

THE IMPACT

The first week of August, three hundred letters and Impact Statement forms were mailed to victims. The questionnaire asked for an explanation of the feelings experienced as a result of this crime, how it affected them personally, including any expense for counseling or therapy. They were asked to give their opinion of whether the person convicted of the crime should pay money for the loss or do work as part of the sentence. These forms, along with the Pre-sentence Investigation Report, were reviewed by the judge prior to sentencing. They enabled representatives to seek a just disposition and sentence in the case.

Judge Nelson utilized his power to advance and promote justice. He was impressed with the comments received:

Please, Judge Nelson, understand our rights.
She used illness to delay us from taking legal action.
We were left out on a limb, and we're still there.
Marsha's calculated and deliberate actions of deceit
*   are inexcusable and should not be tolerated. Give her*
*   the max!*

The Christian assessment was:

She used statements from the Bible. I don't like that.
We have been wounded in our trust in Marsha as a
*   friend. This disturbs me as much as the money loss.*
When I called and asked for a refund, Marsha became

irate. She asked if I was a Christian.

Other comments were:

The stress Marsha caused is measureless.

She caused budget problems.

We had no vacation that year or the next, because we counted on that money.

To say that discovery of this fraudulent action was disappointing would be a gross understatement.

My greatest concern is the lack of remorse and irresponsibility for her lies and deceit.

She corroded my trust in others.

Kathy Hurst said, "In the Marsha Denman case, our office dealt with more victims than any other single-charged crime. Notifying each victim of the upcoming court cases and preparing the numerous victim impact statements that were submitted for the court to review was an opportunity for me to see how one person could cause so much emotional hardship on so many people."

When Tabbey did an arrest warrant, he wasn't sure if Marsha had begun this legitimately and at some point realized it was no longer going to fly, then decided to keep those people's money and induce others fraudulently. He soon discovered, "She never legitimately took any money and then converted it. She took the money fraudulently to begin with. I find what Marsha did in using her religious faith and the testimonials was clearly directed to a designated group of people. In my eyes, she cannot possibly have felt the emotion as she claims in her correspondence. She never would have been able to do that if she was what she claimed to be. It was a pyramid scheme, like a chain letter, where it is designed to fail," he said.

Tabbey figured that after the preliminary examination he would dismiss Count Two, the larceny, which was worthless at that point. He explained that larceny by conversion means that she did not give a false statement to induce you to take the trip, that the trip did

118

exist, what she was telling was true. He said, "But something happened and rather than returning the money she decided to steal it. She had planned to steal from the beginning. She probably thought, *I can't send this out cold, most people would think this doesn't smell right.* She might get a few to bite, but she wasn't going to spend all this time for an insignificant amount of money."

She needed to do two things to make her story somewhat believable. Because $725 seemed very remote, she said, "I have these discounts." Then you question if it's legitimate. If it's on a hand-written piece of paper, no one would buy it, but it would look official on computer-generated documents. I was impressed when I noticed that she created a signature line and a separate set of corporate identifying numbers with another name signed on each receipt to indicate there was someone in the agency working with her. It looked official, but Discount Network Travel only existed in her own mind. There's none in Michigan.

Tabbey said, "There was a signature, S. Daws on these receipts. When all this was collapsing on Marsha, she claimed, 'Sarah Daws is a friend from the church and from General Motors Institute who had the money when I was out of town. She was to turn it over to Laura Muguerza at Travel Agents International.' A subsequent investigation with friends and pastors in the area could not identify Sarah Daws. A history check from the Michigan Drivers License Bureau and Social Security office revealed that Sarah Dawe or Daws is a non-existent person."

Tabbey shared his theory of the case. "She started off with an elaborate scheme, trying to make it look legitimate, but that still won't be convincing enough unless she started with her friends at the church. She got brochures from a travel agency, copied and mailed them to hand-picked prominent members of the church who were not only trustworthy, but people who would believe without question or hesitation. She abused her relationship with church members. This singular insidious tactic has been cited over and over by victims of this crime as the single most important reason why she was able to rob thousands of dollars, while shaking the foundations of their Christian fellowship.

"She needed them to provide testimonials that she is real, so she started the Nashville trips, took money from the Alaskan cruise, and cashed it all out. She had a lot of cash and within six months she was paying over $18,000 directly to the travel agency, when she only charged passengers $250 with a $25 post trip rebate. The trips cost $800 each person, yet the travel agent had no knowledge of what was being charged—they assumed the full rate. Marsha did not reveal the true cost to the people. She controlled the receipts. That was her way to deceive both the travel agency and the people going on the trip. She now had testimonials from eighteen different highly important and respected people.

"Everyone started talking and it mushroomed to multiple states. It was not uncommon for people to send a check for $10,000 to $15,000 for friends and family. Marsha began to enjoy herself at that point. She had not even begun to book any trips to Alaska. She had no contact with any travel agency or Princess Cruise Lines—no bookings whatsoever. As things moved through 1993 and she claimed the trips were scheduled, she had no idea of when they were.

"She got into 1994 realizing that she hadn't booked trips. On May 20, she sent a 10 percent hold to start the process. May ended and June came with faxes, phone calls from the travel agency requesting money from Marsha, or this trip would be canceled. She realized she must cancel the trip when TAI asked for names to send ship documents. Marsha refused to give names.

"On the second page it said, *No air fare*, and a customer sent $725 to TAI, who called Marsha saying, 'What's this?' Marsha wouldn't answer the question.

"The Computer Crime Task Force printed three books from her computer. TAI was not mentioned. She was tripped up from a TAI card that was not on the computer, but found in other records in her basement. Even though there was no paper trail, or money amounts on her computer, her customer [victim] lists and computer forms and letters betrayed her," Tabbey said.

She changed the dates of trips early in 1994, when the travel agency kept bugging her. She had the agency get a schedule and itinerary of all the cruises. She randomly assigned a number of people and informed the agency that she was going to book 165 cabins for 350 people on four different cruises. She only talked about the July 1994 cruise. When she received information, she realized that the starting dates and ending dates were different, and she had to make changes in her confirmation numbers.

In July, the people had an option to either obtain a refund or continue on with new cruises. Marsha made it very inviting to continue on. Many people wanted a refund. Out of nowhere she sent cashier's checks and money orders by Priority Mail. Some got checks, which could be traced easier than cash, although still a difficult task.

A review of Marsha's correspondence with victims revealed that in July and August, she tried to defuse as much as she could, the loudest complainers, the squeaky wheels that gave her problems, and returned at least $71,000. More money was coming in, but it was starting to dry up. In an attempt to defray more angry complaints, she sent out a letter saying all cruises had been canceled and that Princess Cruise Lines would honor and give more perks. She told victims to deal directly with Princess and she would be out of it by March 1995. Tabbey thought that might also mean *out of the country* by March 1995.

In the middle of July when the "Dear Christian Friends" letter came out, all but one trip had been canceled. That was a trip that Marsha didn't even know was going to be booked She had given

$15,000 to Princess Cruise Lines and as each trip failed to be booked, that money was transferred to the next series of trips, eventually building up the deposit.

The last trip was for ten people, going from 165 cabins down to five. There was $15,000 on account at Princess Cruise Lines for one trip, or two thirds the cost required, so they applied it and booked the only Alaska trip for ten people in September. After all other trips were being canceled and Marsha was blaming it on the fictitious Sarah Daws, the travel agency said, "Marsha we have the trip in July. You need to pay the remaining amount of money in order to secure full booking." Marsha applied $6,000 and the trip was booked at over $21,000 for ten people. That meant that the trip cost over $2,100 per person.

At this time the house of cards was collapsing. Marsha had been cut off from her disability at GMI and the insurance company that was holding the long term disability was canceling. She was not getting sufficient money. Her regular income was rapidly disappearing. The other trips had been canceled, and there was no way now that she could justify to the people about the trips. She scrambled to figure out what to do.

She had finished taking her year of fun trips, (eight vacations from May 1993 to May 1994), and realized that much of the money had been funneled into the hands of others. She needed to come up with the money and hold off as many people as she could from complaining to the Attorney General. Many complaints had been filed at this point.

"What occurred, happened rapidly," Tabbey said. "She was out of money. She didn't spend all of the money. We don't know where it is, but it wasn't in the banks or anything we could find. She would take it to cash.

"In August 1994, she tried to obtain a number of loans. She went to Security Federal Credit Union to get a personal loan for $10,000; that was denied. She tried to obtain a loan from between

$80,000 and $200,000 from Mr. Floyd Echart, a mechanical contractor in the area. When he inquired as to who needed this money, what were her assets, how would it be paid off, she implicated herself, refused to give information and declined to continue with that attempt.

"Hurting for money, Marsha waited a day or so, then sent a letter canceling the last and only trip scheduled asking TAI to have Princess Cruise Lines send the refund to her. When the material came in to give to these people, [ten people who didn't even know they were booked], it was the same time everything else was collapsing. Prior to canceling, the travel agency received knowledge of letters and faxes where people were clamoring for refunds of their $725 trip cost. They told Marsha they would not give the information to her, but would send it directly to the people. Marsha realized that those people would have seen the cost of the trip and their first question would be, who is paying for the rest of this trip? Am I going to be liable?

"I believe Marsha's original plan was to skate out from underneath this, and eventually shift it all on to Princess Cruise Lines and when everyone turned their heads to look there, she would slip out of town. Maybe I'm giving her too much credit, but it appears to me that the only way to get out of this was to leave this jurisdiction. People would have turned their heads right back, once they contacted Princess and they disavowed any knowledge of this. She was trying to open a window of opportunity to escape and get away from all this, where attention would be turned away from her. It didn't happen. We arrested her.

"Marsha finally made her first realistic decision that there was no way she could fight this case; that she would be found guilty. Whether she has the wherewithal to anticipate how many problems she now will face, I can't give her credit for that. Up to this point, she has been in total denial or in the form of self-delusion. People that get involved in these frauds convince themselves of their own lies and they start believing that everything's going to be okay. This belief is not based on reality.

"The last week before trial, there were indications that Marsha wanted to have her counsel serve a dozen people with subpoenas for being character witnesses, which would have been a bad move on the part of the defense, because the prosecution can ask each one, in succession, about the things she did and if that would change their opinion. Most of them would change their opinion or at least be shocked and want to disbelieve it. The prosecution could tell their story, by asking the same questions and the jury would hear it over and over again. Apparently she decided against that and the course of action was the plea," Tabbey said.

On Friday before trial date, Marsha's attorney, out of courtesy, told the prosecution that it was his impression that Marsha was going to plead but not that day. Sometimes that's a bluff to get the prosecution to drop their guard. On the other hand, it only made them work harder over the weekend to get ready. Tabbey believes if you're prepared and ready to go you'll most likely get a plea. It's sort of an old prosecutor adage.

Ms. Lloyd, Siegel and Tabbey spent from 1 P.M. Saturday until 3 A.M. Sunday preparing dollar amounts and dates for the audit. They were doing multiple tasks in getting the file ready for trial, however, the audit was the key turning point in the case. Tabbey said, "Not only did it expose Marsha to the undeniable lies that she took money from the beginning, but it exposed her family and friends to a great multitude of questions about what they knew, when they knew it, and why didn't they do something about it."

"Her parents were supportive until the day of the plea, July 31, 1995, when it seemed that they weren't right with Marsha. Perhaps they were more relieved that she pled due to the enlightenment they had over the weekend, audit facts showing large sums of money received from Marsha. On the stand, Sgt. Siegel would expose and identify her parents and her sister Lori, who received thousands of dollars. Then he would identify her boyfriend. I'm not certain if it started off as her sister's boyfriend and then her live-in boyfriend, but Brad Younce received several thousand dollars."

The parents were embarrassed that family, friends and church friends would be looking at them with much more serious question. I think it was a relief to them that it didn't have to come out dramatically in a jury trial. Combined pressure of the audit and preparation on the rest of the matters showing that the prosecution had people ready to talk, finally culminated in the realization that the trial would also expose her friends and family members to full public scrutiny.

The audit made it impossible for Marsha to defend herself because it exposed her on every angle. The jury would question where the money was. There's no way she could answer that question. She would have to tell everybody why she wrote checks to her mom and dad and to friends and explain how she could take trips and spend a hundred thousand dollars of money on a gross income of $20,000 in 1993, and $6,592 in 1994. How could she explain her extravagant lifestyle? Obviously, she could not, without confessing the truth.

On Thursday, Tabbey told the defense he would prepare another audit chart with large boxes showing how much money came in to Marsha, what her legitimate income was and where she spent it. The dollar amounts would be visible throughout the whole trial, for the jury to inspect. He knew this would produce a tremendous impact, and was able to finally convince her of the strength in the case against her.

On Friday, prior to the trial date, Tabbey spent four hours going through bank records. He could trace the money, starting with the Vollers' where she washed more than $200,000, to the collapse of her enterprise in August 1994. Tabbey pointed out to the defense, "The money is coming in and going directly out. She's bleeding the accounts dry. It wasn't in a bank account. It didn't go to any travel agency."

On the morning of the scheduled trial, I observed Marsha's stunned expression as she saw that the prosecution came in with everything they said they had, hundreds of documents marked and ready to go. The audit entries started on September 14, 1992, at the Flint Area School Employees Credit Union. The first entry was designated as the Voller check for $8,337.50, which came in for the Alaskan cruise. Marsha deposited $2,000 of that check and took out in cash, that day, $6,337.50. Her GMI payroll check came in for $622 so she now had $2,600 in that account. A few days later she withdrew $2,300, $200, $125, bleeding the account to a small amount of money.

Her next biweekly payroll check was deposited. She withdrew another $500, then more money came in, $16,000 for another series of Voller checks. She immediately withdrew $4,000 in cash, deposited $12,500. The next day she took out $2,500. The next day she wrote a check for $9,200 to pay off her car.

She made a deposit of $9,200 which was a loan from her credit union. The next day she drained all of the Voller money, and everything left in that account. Her next payroll came in, and additional checks were deposited. Then she immediately drained the account.

She continued this pattern until the account was closed in 1994. She either took money when she deposited it (or within the next few days) and drained the account mostly in cash, some in money orders. Many were official checks. That's how the investigators traced her two car purchases, the money to her friends and relatives, rent and an average payment of $160-$200 phone bills per month. She spent $17,500 on her Visa account for a seven-month period.

I believe the only reason a person systematically depletes their account is they know that at any given time this could collapse and they don't want to lose everything. The pattern was clearly established. If the money had been legitimately there, why wasn't it still there and why didn't the trail go from her account to a check to Princess Cruise Lines or to TAI for payment on these cruises?

Tabbey displayed earnest concern when he said, "I don't like it when nest eggs are taken, leaving retirees in their golden years without any funds and assets forcing them to rely on Social Security and Medicare when they were going to enjoy a fine retirement. Many are senior citizens who have lived a good life, paid taxes, only to have everything taken from them. In this case it wasn't everything, but it certainly would hurt most seniors to lose $725 a person not to mention the shattered dreams.

"I feel like the justice system right now is inadequate to deal with schemers like Marsha. I have prosecuted computer hackers, quite a number of scams in the hundreds of thousands of dollars, attorneys and insurance brokers stealing from their clients, telemarketers stealing from their investors. Marsha Denman stealing from people in her own religious faith. We're barely able to keep up with the violent criminals, who need in many cases, to just be warehoused, because they'll just come out and do the same thing.

"So what do you do with a person like Marsha Denman who in the state of Michigan, no matter how many counts I brought, faces a maximum of ten years imprisonment? Her sentencing guidelines are very low. They don't account for the magnitude of this fraud. To do at least what I believe is a proper sentence, the judge has to go well over the guidelines and in many cases that I have prosecuted where the courts have gone well over the guidelines on frauds, the court would give a sentence in our department of corrections, which means approximately six months behind bars before they are put on a tether. It's just not much time. That's why I felt from the beginning that I had to do this as a joint prosecution with the Federal authorities," he said.

The needs of the out-of-state victims cannot adequately be addressed by the Jackson County prosecution. Federally, mail fraud counts are stackable offenses. They have a different set of guidelines that in this case will be consecutive, after Michigan sentencing. In Michigan, the court can issue a restitution order for all victims, but it still doesn't provide enough protection for them to get their money back.

In one case, a very good attorney put a stay on the Michigan proceedings, went directly to Federal court, did what they call a rule eleven plea agreement saying, 'I'll plead to one, if you don't charge me with multiple counts of mail fraud, and I'll agree to do two years in the Federal penitentiary.' He agreed to do that and was sentenced by that court prior to the case coming up for sentencing in Washtenaw County. Therefore, they avoided a consecutive sentence, since the Federal case was done first and Michigan law doesn't demand that it be consecutive. Marsha's delay is going to cost her. That's why Michigan wanted to deal with her first.

If a civil suit is successful it would give victims the benefit of a judgment that would last ten years, renewable for at least another ten. There is no way to say it can be lifted because they can't pay. It is at least a twenty-year option to collect. A class action suit could be easily created by those from across the country who paid money to Marsha Denman.

Research reveals that white collar offenses are neglected by State prosecutors. In most fraud cases the money will never be found or returned, and many of these individuals will do their best to get as short a sentence as possible.

In August, the postal inspector and the Internal Revenue Service met with Tabbey who affirmed, "The IRS wants its taxes because it's obvious from just that one audit that Marsha earned a couple hundred thousand dollars. We saw her tax records from our search warrant. She didn't indicate that she earned that kind of money. All she reported is what she earned at General Motors Institute. Marsha has a lot of problems with the IRS.

"It was apparent from investigation, that she deceived her employer, GMI. On her employment application she claimed she had college credits when she had none. She started in the mid 80s as a clerk; worked her way up until about 1992 when her tax records and W2 form showed earned gross pay of about $19,000 as a clerk typist. She had occasion to call a travel agent that worked exclusively with GMI, but that was not her main duty. The travel agent handled the arrangements. That's where she became interested in the travel business.

"Records retrieved by search warrant from GMI showed she was acceptable as an employee. They gave her good reviews, but she wasn't satisfied. She wanted a raise. From then on her life was not too good. In 1993, she experienced physical health problems. She started to write in sick quite a bit, allegedly falsifying physician's records to get time off. She was drawing unemployment from GMI. Although the records on October 6, 1993, show she was sick, she was in Toronto on one of her trips. That's one reason she was fired in January 1995. Medical records from GMI were subpoenaed. Those records showed she had rheumatoid arthritis, not lupus or multiple sclerosis as she claimed."

~ CHAPTER ELEVEN ~

SENTENCING

I will always remember the dramatic day, September 27, 1995, in Judge Charles Nelson's court. The front row was occupied by Marsha, her casually dressed parents, Lori, Brad and a large built dark haired male. Lori put her arm around Marsha who looked calm, sullen and somber, in her black jacket and skirt, purple blouse, flat shoes and no makeup.

Judge Nelson took care of two sentences, a defendant with four prior felonies for larceny over $100, and a criminal who promised never to become involved in drugs again.

Hurst and Tabbey took their place at the prosecution table. Rappleye appeared on the scene a few minutes later. He and Marsha left the room to review the Pre-sentence Investigation interview. They returned as the bailiff was refusing a Detroit TV news reporter's request to set up equipment. He had not filed a seven-day prior request.

Siegel was in school so he sent an eight-page letter to the judge, who shuffled papers on his desk and asked Attorney Rappleye if he had any questions, comments, additions or deletions, and if he had reviewed the Pre-sentence Investigation Report.

Rappleye stood and said he had two or three comments. "Regarding Ms. Denman's health, they make note of the fact that she suffers from a serious illness. Those conclusions are supported by medical reports from the University of Michigan medical staff in Ann Arbor. They don't say what should be done. It is our position that although poor health would not excuse any criminal activity, certainly jails and/or units of incarceration aren't very well qualified to deal with those health problems."

Marsha's lips were pointed and stern, a pouting look. She stood next to Rappleye, hands folded. She blinked often, glared at the floor then gave Rappleye a severe look as if to reprimand. Mr. Denman jiggled his foot, crossed and uncrossed his legs, and twisted his mouth as he put an arm around his wife. Lori bit her nails while her companion appeared to be unruffled. Hurst and Tabbey compared notes.

Rappleye leaned intensely on the podium, carefully read his notes and pushed on, "Restitution has been made in excess of $100,000 and taking that fact against trooper Siegel's very vitriolic letter, if Ms. Denman is guilty of 5 percent of the malice and maliciousness that he accuses her of, she could have made a deposit in the Grand Cayman Islands or somewhere else and it wouldn't be available for restitution. You don't make restitution if you have an intent to defraud and to steal, etc.

"This situation arose because of some poor business practices. Ms. Denman started dumping this money into her personal account and it wasn't long until she used money for the wrong purposes. Regarding statements about remorse or admitting to any wrong doing, both of those statements are wrong. She does have remorse about this, and she certainly represents to the court that she has fault, and that the fault lies with no one else other than herself. So we would request, Your Honor, that she be placed on a term of probation in order to make restitution. She has demonstrated the ability to make restitution in a substantial amount. It's my judgment that given the opportunity she could make all of the so-called travelers or travelees, whatever, whole in this matter."

The judge asked Rappleye, "Do you agree with the figure of $350,597.50?"

Marsha shook her head, looked at Rappleye as he replied, "No sir. We think it's about $100,000 less."

"What do you have to show me that it's $100,000 less?"

"I think Ms. Denman's testimony, if she were allowed to testify. I don't have any documents. They were seized by the search warrant and we don't have access to them."

"So you can see at least $250,000?"

"Yes."

The judge asked Marsha if she had any comments. There was a heavy pause of several seconds as the word "comments" settled in.

"Yes," she answered while approaching the podium. She clutched a large sheet of paper in her hand.

She must have a lot to say, I thought. *This is the moment we've been waiting for.* It was an emotionally charged time for the victims who had wondered if Marsha would speak during any of the court sessions, and if she would admit guilt. Showing no emotion, she exhaled and calmly began reading:

"Your Honor and those within this courtroom, I'd like to take this opportunity to say how truly sorry I am for any heartache this situation has caused. From the day I canceled the trip in question, your well-being has been my concern and prayer. Though it may be hard for you to understand, God knows what was and is, in my heart as he does with each person sitting in this courtroom.

"At this time, over $160,000 has been reimbursed, $75,000 of that soon after cancellation. I have no doubt in my mind that the remainder will be compensated as promised. I'd like to also thank those who have shown a true Christ-like spirit through their support, perhaps in prayer, kind words, a smile or hug. You'll never know how much those meant to me, but I fully intend on sharing with others in need.

"Please continue to keep my family and friends and I, in your prayers as we do you. Thank you for opening your ears and your heart and listening to this statement. May God bless each one of you."

Victims had listened to that friendly, persuasive voice many times. The words, "Your well-being has been my concern and prayer," kept bounding around inside my head. Her speech sounded rehearsed. She seemed to be convincing herself that what she was saying was the truth. The judge watched her carefully. She returned to her seat as an observer whispered, "Still using Christianity." The victims agreed.

Hurst stood and said, "Your Honor, we'd like to begin the presentation of the state of Michigan with two of the victims who are here to testify to the court."

"Your Honor, I think this might take a long time, may we sit down?" Rappleye requested.

Judge Nelson answered, "You may." He handed a folder to the court clerk, looked at Hurst and said, "Mr. Hurst, I have read your statements dated September 22 and September 26, and also Trooper Siegel's report. I should mention that I have received numerous letters on behalf of Ms. Denman, which I've reviewed, plus the prosecutor's office has done excellent tabulation with regard to losses, names of victims and impact statements which have been reviewed."

Hurst continued. "It's our request this morning, our intention that the two victims who wish to make oral impact statements enlighten the court from their perspective. This is Pat Lively who is here to speak."

Although I was unaccustomed to facing a judge, I found satisfaction in the expectation of voicing my views. Hurst and Tabbey, with whom I had hashed over the facts of this case, sat on my left, while four feet separated me from Marsha and her attorney who sat snugly on my right. I stood tall (no pun intended for my 5 foot 2 inch physique) glanced at my notes, smiled at Judge Nelson and on behalf of 156 Jackson County victims, 161 in the state of Michigan, and 256 in other states, I began:

"Your Honor: Our dreams of an anniversary cruise ended in bitter awakenings."

Pointing to the 4- by 6-foot audit chart I said, "As seen in the preliminary hearings, this audit chart showed checks Marsha wrote to drama clubs, relatives and friends. Money was spent for cars, Visa bills, elegant trips and rent for her condo. Marsha washed a half-million dollars through bank accounts between 1992 and 1994, more money than many victims will ever see.

"She used Christianity as a tool for her contemptible crime. On July 10, 1994, her 'Dear Christian Friends' letter stated that she talked with cruise lines and she had approval and a confirmation number directly from the cruise lines; that they would send the money to her and upon receipt she would immediately or within six to eight weeks, forward it to each person that paid for the cruise. This was one of the many promises to repay the victims.

"In one letter she said 'With God's help, the expected lengthy illness which I will suffer, will be a blessing in disguise.' Stickers on Marsha's correspondence said, 'God is Love.' I wonder, does Marsha believe that God is love? When God's children break the rules, He is hurt and disappointed, just like we are. Marsha put tears in God's eyes.

"The coordinator trusted Marsha. The people involved trusted the coordinator. My husband and I invited others to accompany us on a ship that didn't sail. Many victims are on a fixed income. Some are still paying interest on money sent to Marsha.

"A dear friend of mine who had invested in Europe and Alaska trips, was so distraught he suffered a fatal heart attack two weeks after the scam was uncovered.

"Why were some of the victims fortunate enough to receive a refund and some of us did not recover our loss? How was the decision made as to who would be paid and who would be forgotten, just marked off the list? Where did the money go?

"In essence, Marsha committed over five hundred robberies by coming into our homes through the computer, the mail and the telephone.

"Marsha should be forced to repay every dime to the victims. One week's vacation is what she promised us. We paid *her* for one week. She should serve time—one week for every victim she failed to repay. She has already had a year to make amends.

"She should serve one year of community service, by assisting those on a fixed income. Maybe that would teach her what it's like to skimp and save."

There was silence in the courtroom except for my nine-minute earnest plea. Hurst and Tabbey stood as I concluded, "Your Honor, I thank you for listening to me." Hurst opened the wooden swinging gate and I returned to the observer's section, feeling I had established that victims have rights. The judge was intent, earnest and did everything in his power to produce restitution.

Hurst thanked me and announced that Carole France would present her Impact Statement.

"Your Honor," she began. "My employer informed me that she was going on an Alaskan cruise which was associated with the Spring Arbor Free Methodist church. My friend Cathy Henry and I wanted to go to Alaska before we retired, so we decided to join the group. I worked two full-time jobs to earn the money to pay for the trip. We sent checks to Marsha Denman with no idea we were being defrauded.

"The literature, letters and confirmation forms which Marsha mailed appeared official. As the date of our trip approached with no tickets, schedule of flights, etc., we wrote Marsha. When we were informed the trip was postponed, she still pretended to be legitimate. My vacation time had been approved and I could not change it. Since the trip was not happening, I took out a loan to take a vacation with Cathy. Nothing like the dream Alaskan cruise, but a trip by car to Ohio for one week.

"My life became a nightmare when I contacted the Michigan State Police to investigate the matter. While I was helping them gather information, there were victims who treated me cruelly because they believed there was no possibility of a crime.

"Marsha Denman has manipulated people, the legal system and my life. My character was subject to untruths suggested by the defense attorney. It was suggested that Mark Siegel and I had met and made up the story.

"Articles that appeared in the local newspapers and television stations subjected me to many comments and remarks from people who felt we were 'stupid' and 'why didn't you use a local travel agent?' It seemed like the whole world knew I had been taken by a con artist.

"Because of the articles in the local newspaper and television, I was contacted at my home by a group of eighteen people in New York who had signed up for one of Marsha's trips and heard there were problems. They wanted information about what was being done. Several notes and newspaper articles were mailed back and forth from this group. They received a refund following an article in the local newspaper about possible Federal charges.

"It was very humiliating to be on the stand to watch Marsha seated at the defense table during the pre-trial hearing, acting as if I was making false accusations about her involvement with the trip and the loss of money.

"When Marsha Denman pleaded no contest at the hearing to which I had been subpoenaed, I was unable to have my day in court to express my outrage and emotional pain.

"My doctor diagnosed me with stress and venules insufficiency. I was off work for several weeks. I was fitted for compression stockings, learned to operate a Lumpha Press that I will need for the rest of my life to help circulation in the lower half of my body. I could have used the refund money to help with the medical service and supplies which was more than $8,000. Since my health has deteriorated, I may never be able to take my dream vacation trip to Alaska.

"It appears that Marsha picks and chooses who and when she will return the money, at times that benefit her most and help her case. I am angry that my money which Marsha has held for months has not been returned. I believe that Marsha Denman should serve time in prison for her crime. Justice should be served for the many hard-working victims. Thank you, Your Honor."

Many victims refused to come forth and present anything about this case. Many were too embarrassed to be seen at the court sessions. But Carole France was the courageous one that began the process, acting on behalf of 572 others. She felt immense emotion the day she went to the prosecutor's office and provided letters and exhibits. She physically relived the events of the last two years when she recalled the humiliating experience for which she was unprepared.

Carole is an intensely private person, deeply wounded, unable to hide the unbearable pain. It was impossible to look at her on the witness stand without feeling compassion. We talked about her day in court. "It was difficult to look at Marsha. It seemed unfair and unreasonable for me to be the one on the stand testifying, when Marsha was the one that fabricated the scam. I was overwhelmed by the fact that it seemed I had to prove more in terms of what happened, than she did.

"When her attorney questioned me, Marsha's behavior revealed denial, indicating that what I was saying was untrue. Rappleye questioned. Marsha shook her head. He cross-examined. She raised her hands. He rephrased questions when she wrote notes on a tablet and whispered in his ear.

"He questioned how long I've known Siegel, when I meet him, how many personal contacts have I had with him. The accusation that trooper Siegel and I conspired all this really got me. I soon figured out while on the witness stand, what they were attempting to do. They wanted to say that this was the prosecution's scheme to catch Marsha in this and that she was the victim of the travel agency taking the money.

"My life became almost as public as Marsha's. I had to tell a lot about myself that I don't normally explain to others. My physical condition became public knowledge because I had to share that, along with my disappointment and loss of money.

"My life has changed. When I get information about travel I tear it up, even if it sounds good. I don't want to be involved in travel plans again. My trust has been completely destroyed. I'm more investigative, more skeptical, take more thought about doing anything.

"I was subpoenaed on a murder case. After the hearing and sentencing, one of the men that was sentenced wrote in the newspaper opinion page about prosecuting the wrong person, that he was a Christian and he wasn't guilty. This brought Marsha to mind. I'm angered by the gall Marsha has. I believe Marsha was into the scam the very instant she received the first check. She did the crime, but doesn't want to do the time," she said.

Hurst thanked Ms. France and swiftly stood up. "I'd like to comment regarding the presentation of the defense. He indicated to the court that if Marsha's guilty, and was as malicious as referred in Sgt. Siegel's letter, she'd go to the Cayman Islands. The fact of the matter is $497,000 was taken; $146,000 was refunded through the process as part of the scam, and $350,000 is missing. It's either in the Cayman Islands or somewhere. And only Marsha Denman knows where it is. The defense counsel says she's truly responsible for all this harm that's been done, putting money into a personal account and started using it on her own."

He placed an audit chart on the easel, pointed out each entry as he talked. "When she took the first check to the bank on September

14, 1992, for $8,337 from the Voller family, she took it right out. She started using it moments later. The defense respectfully disagrees that $350,000 is still outstanding and if Marsha had the records she could testify to that. He's exactly correct. We have the records. The search warrant and seized records have helped us prove to the court what she did, who was cheated and how much money was lost.

"These fraud crimes are white collar crimes, often not taken seriously by some of the law enforcement process—economic crimes. No one is beaten and bleeding when the police arrived, no one shot, no one's home has been violated. It's just money and can be replaced. It's not a life. That's not all of the story in this case. It doesn't tell the real tragedy that occurred for these victims. As these victims told us, it's about families, their future, a healthy community, dream-come-true vacations and perhaps most importantly, the concepts of faith and trust in your fellow man and woman. That was destroyed here. White collar crimes are a very serious matter. Many are senior citizens, widows and widowers, and that faith and trust that Christian people hold dear, will never recover from this offense.

"The circuit court, probation office and defense had the opportunity to review the hundreds of impact statements. Those victim impact statements describe more adequately and more clearly the permanent impact of this crime, than almost any set of impact statements I've ever seen. They're honest, hard working, decent people who know how to put their thoughts into writing to the judge.

"Many criminals who come before this court have harmed only one or two persons or maybe themselves or their families, but not this defendant. This defendant stands before the court having harmed 573 victims and their families in this scheme. On the morning of trial we would have presented exhibits to the court showing how easily this scam took place. It happened through Marsha's shrewd use of a personal computer."

Many victims readily recalled the next exhibit. "She used letters like this dated September 13, 1993, in which she said to the victims, 'I called the travel agency to verify.' That's not true. There was no travel agent. She said 'the normal charge is $1,450 but with my discount, the cost is only $725. This amount is payable to me,' she said, and she issued her receipts."

Hurst never backed away, but held his ground, continuously maintained eye contact. "Then she caused the most pain when she said, 'I'm from the Davison Free Methodist church and I'm enthused over the fact that a large majority of the Voller group are Christians.' She used Christianity to prey on them. She has issued receipts from Network Travel. Network Travel never existed. She said, 'It was applied within our agency toward your Alaskan adventure.' Conveniently, here's a signature under Network Travel and this person doesn't even exist."

Hurst turned toward the audience, paced a few extra steps to replace the exhibit with a larger one. He stirred another recollection and coolly pointed out, "After numerous people who had paid for these trips never received tickets, they started contacting her. Then she started writing letters where the apologies and lies began to mushroom. She always used this salutation, 'Dear Christian Friend.' She said she used one travel agency and had to switch to another, but we found she never used a single travel agent; then a lot of other mumbo jumbo in her letter.

"She then said, 'I will keep a close monitor on each refund. There's no problem in obtaining the refund amounts.' She promised a refund fourteen months ago. Then when victims became insistent, she told them Princess Cruise Lines has agreed to honor the discount and Princess Cruise Lines will issue tickets after March 1995. They'll bail you out. To Marsha, March 1995 is a significant date. Princess Cruise Lines was going to handle it and she was starting to bail out with all that money!"

He placed a new exhibit on the easel. His hand gestures became more apparent, producing horizontal, vertical and circular motions, as though this case had enveloped his whole being. "This form is a Princess Cruise Lines confirmation. I'm quite certain that when Carole France received this in July 1994, she thought it was a confirmation and the trip was going to occur. Marsha should have known that people would contact Princess Cruise Lines. People contacted Princess Cruise Lines and they responded in writing, 'I have reviewed your letter and was very sorry to learn that you have done business with Marsha Denman.' Marsha never dealt with them. That was another lie.

"When the Michigan State Police began to arrive with the prosecuting attorney's search warrants, then came the letters about refunds and illness and what a bad guy Sgt. Siegel was. Sgt. Siegel, the man that cracked this case." The next exhibit showed a neatly drafted replica of Marsha's honey-dripping words. Hurst went on, "She said, 'I wanted to write you a note to thank you for the patience you've shown while waiting for the return of your cruise money.' She talked about the media, and checking into the background of persons who wear a badge. She had the gall to say, 'You will find that Trooper Siegel is dishonest. I would have no concern about refunding your money. I'm refunding the money as promised after my attorney approves it. The Lord knows the truth, as does Sgt. Siegel, and I, for one, am not afraid to see Him on judgment day.' He looked in Marsha's direction and emphatically declared, "Today is judgment day for Marsha Denman."

Hurst Placed a new exhibit on the easel and pointed out, "This, Your Honor, is computerized forms, *Explore Europe without exploiting your bank account.* The People suggest, Your Honor, that it was Marsha Denman doing all the exploiting. Marsha Denman used Woody Voller, former president of Spring Arbor

College, now deceased, to vouch for her credibility that she was an outstanding person. Mr. Voller himself, a great man in this area, was ensnared in her trap by the trip she put together for Nashville to get everybody, including Woody Voller's friends, interested in her scheme.

"She continued to run a classic show game. She promised refunds, then when she couldn't make refunds she blamed people around her. She blamed the travel agency. That didn't work. Then she blamed the Michigan State Police and her attorney who had to approve the refunds."

Hurst continued talking as he displayed the large audit chart. "Through the Computer Crime Task Force, chaired by Sgt. Peplinski and Mr. Tabbey from our office, using this exhibit known as Forensic Accounting, we found out where she got the money. Over one hundred hours went into reconstructing where she got the money and where she spent it. It has been pointed out to the court that $13,000 went to her parents Larry and Shirley Denman. Large sums of money went to Bradley Younce, a 22-year-old boyfriend.

"Marsha began taking trips and buying expensive automobiles. As Sgt. Siegel indicated, despite all this money, not one person ever stepped on a plane or a boat except Marsha Denman. She took trips to Minneapolis with her sister, trips to Cedar Point, Denver, Chicago, Toronto, Orlando and Minneapolis again. These trips were usually first class, fancy limousines and automobiles, expensive meals and lots of other finery that her victims never received. She bought two expensive automobiles, a Pontiac Bonneville and a Buick Regal, at the time she was taking money from these people."

Lori hung her head, bit her nails. Her partner put his arm around her. He whispered in her ear. Marsha carefully watched Hurst, who paced in her direction, but returned to the podium. "She knew exactly what she was doing. She maintained to the victims that the Michigan State Police falsely accused her. On the day of trial, July 31, 1995, in this courtroom when she had a chance to showcase her innocence and how wrong the Michigan State Police were, she ponied up to the court with a plea as charged, larceny by false pretenses.

"Our records show she took $497,000 which is clearly one of Michigan history's most successful robberies. Apparently, she entered the plea thinking no one would find out how much money was taken and how many victims were involved. That's where she bumped up against the Michigan State Police and the Computer Crime Task Force, using her records, who found how much she received and how much she took."

The prosecutor's face firmed, became flushed and the tone of voice sharpened with each fact pointed out. He became more emotional as he spoke. "We're here today, Your Honor, because now it's time for the truth. The truth is, Marsha L. Denman stole a half million dollars. The truth is, she still owes $350,000. The truth is also shown, that she used money to live like a queen, extensively traveling first class, at the expense of her victims. The truth is she's a thief and one of the worst in Michigan's history."

Hurst glanced at Marsha, looked at the judge and pointed out in an aggressive manner, "She not only lied to the victims, because when she prepared to stand before Your Honor to answer for her crimes, her lies continued and are well documented in the Pre-sentence Investigation Report.

"Not only did we determine that this woman cheated six hundred people, but she has cheated others. She told Diana Sinclair that she had earned seventy-two credits at Mott Community College. There is no record that she ever attended.

"She was fired after almost ten years when her employer learned she was falsifying time-keeping records and a medical disability claim. She told her employer she was sick on a certain day and it was learned that she was in Toronto on vacation. Another day she said she was sick and it was learned that she was on Mackinac Island. She claimed illness. She scammed her employer, said she was sick, filed medical disability forms with her employer, but guess what? On the doctor's portion of the form, his name was signed by none other than Marsha Denman. She wasn't disabled. She was scamming her employer and the insurance company and she got away with it for years."

Marsha's lips twisted, her glasses slipped down on her nose. She looked at the floor. She watched Hurst sideways as he laid the facts out for everyone to see and hear. Rappleye looked through his papers.

Hurst persisted, "So because she continues to maintain her innocence Your Honor, this court has to hand this woman a sentence which will definitely wake her up to what she has done and a lengthy prison term to think about the pre-meditated and calculating of what she did to these people. Some of them are in the courtroom today.

"The court has seen comments from victims who indicated their grief, disgust and shame. They are very disappointed about what she had done to them. As we have indicated to the court, Marsha L. Denman has proven that she is the Michigan version of Jim Bakker. One of the victims has said that this woman cheated 573 victims and should receive one week for every person she cheated. That is an honest assessment of what should happen to her. After all, one victim indicated, she promised us one week, she should serve one week in return. After $500,000 not one victim stepped on a boat or plane. Another victim indicated that this woman collected more in two years than most of the victims will ever see in an entire lifetime."

Hurst declared, "Your Honor, she had the chance to come to court today with that pile of money in her hand. She didn't bring it because she spent it. We ask for full restitution as a condition of parole, and a prison sentence for one of the largest robberies in Michigan history, six years, eight months minimum, ten years maximum. Thank you."

144

Hurst left the podium with the knowledge that the prosecution had challenged everything that Marsha had said. He took it personally that she had taken advantage of numerous individuals in the community, painting the picture of senior citizens on a limited income, and the fact that she misused people who did family things, and insulted their belief in Christianity.

When the judge asked Rappleye if he had any comments, he coughed, cleared his throat and said, "Uh, uh, counsel says that Ms. Denman didn't have any contact with a travel agency. As a matter of fact, they confiscated an $8,000 check from that same travel agency, so I think Mr. Hurst ought to get his facts straight in that regard."

The judge clarified, "That's with regard to just ten reservations?"

Rappleye answered, "Yes. Thanks very much."

Judge Nelson removed his glasses and stated tersely, "It appears that we have here a classic Ponzi scheme that started with trips to Nashville at below cost, such a good deal that people couldn't pass up the next deal that came along. It's easy to understand how a person could get sucked into the good deal. People were easily led from one trip into the other. It certainly appears that this scheme did result in a significant amount of money going to the defendant for which she has not made any accounting yet. The many letters written on behalf of Ms. Denman refer to her great Christianity and her Christian ties."

But the judge counteracted Marsha's request for leniency by using scripture. "The comments about the great trips that I'm going to give you reminds one of the statement in James:

> *Even so the tongue is a little member and boasts of great things. Behold how great a matter a little fire kindleth and the tongue is a fire in a world of iniquity.*

*So is the tongue among our member that defileth the
whole body and setteth on fire the course of nature and
is set on fire of hell.*

"It appears that her little member has caused a lot of hell with
the victims in this case. People on Social Security who don't have
money to waste on these trips. People on limited income have had
their lives significantly affected. This type of scheme has to be
protected and deterred by Marsha L. Denman and others.

"A major element beyond punishment is trying to secure
restitution. Restitution becomes a difficult matter because she's
spent beyond $80,000 for various trips, etc. A lot of the money has
been spent and frittered away. It's a question as to what, if anything, we can do to try to get some of the people's money back.
She's 39, fired from her last job for fraud. We have to realize no
one's going to get their money back. If she's incarcerated she can't
work.

"In terms of what she wishes to do with her life, I'm going to
provide to counsel two alternative sentences. Ms. Denman will be
back here on November 15 at eight-thirty in the morning. It will be
up to her as to which one she gets. If she pays $250,000 by No-
vember 8, 1995, to be placed in trust fund to partially repay the
victims, I'll place her on 48 months probation.

"If she fails to pay that money by November 15, she will serve
a minimum term of 48 months to the maximum term of 120
months, credit for one day, at the Michigan Department of Corrections. This is an upward departure from the guidelines that are set
forth in view of the number of victims, in view of the nature of this
crime, in view of the necessity to deter and protect society from
computer crime. It is recommended by the probation department
and the amount of restitution will be made a condition of parole,
but I think everyone has to realize that's going to be rather mean-
ingless.

"She should write a letter of apology to each victim, she shall not be involved in travel business, she shall perform 250 hours of community service, pay $40 to criminal right's fund, $960 supervision fee at $20 a month.

Rappleye questioned, "Your Honor, for clarification, can the $8,000 be used for reimbursements?"

The judge replied, "No, $200,000 should be on top of that."

Hurst quickly stood to his feet and stated, "Thank you, I believe so, as well."

Judge Nelson finalized the day: "$8,500 is setting at Travel Agents International to be disbursed. I'm giving you copies of the sentences. We'll be back November 15."

Court adjourned at ten, thus ending another day where we found out that if Marsha doesn't pay, Judge Nelson will book a trip of his own for her—to a state prison for at least four years.

Mel complimented the prosecutors on the course of action taken. Hurst said, "Marsha's lawyer did a fine job for her, but lawyers can't change the facts. It's disingenuous that she has suggested now that her lawyer didn't do his job."

Marsha, surrounded by family members, hurried away from the building, declining comment to news media, which was in the hallway, full force.

I gave a press statement that the experience had strengthened my faith, and we can't give up on humanity because we made a mistake in trusting a person. Hurst added, "She tried to scam the judge, but he didn't go for it. He stood his ground. And that's where it stopped—with the judge."

Friends in Florida read the Associated Press release that gave a clear, accurate account of one of the largest robberies in Michigan's history.

Weeks passed with no word regarding a refund. On a cool October afternoon, the scent of cinnamon apple crisp wafted through the house as it baked. Grandchildren Nathan, Lauren, Lindsay and I raked the autumn leaves into a mound ready for tumbling, raking and tumbling again. It was a melancholy task, for it reminded me of many afternoons when we'd done the same chore. We sat at the picnic table to rest while we talked about the past summer. Nathan said, "Grandma, will you and Grandpa ever take that trip to Alaska?"

"We haven't heard anything about the money Marsha promised a month ago," I said. "The weather's turned chilly, fall is here, winter is coming, O.J. is a free man, Clinton has started campaigning for next year, and not one red cent has rolled into the victims' mailboxes. Nothing. Zip. I'm trying to forget Alaska. Let's have dessert," I suggested. They readily accepted my offer.

~ CHAPTER TWELVE ~
RESERVATIONS CONFIRMED

A lawyer doesn't need to love his client or believe in his legal or moral innocence. Over and above that fact, I still had questions: How did Rappleye feel about Marsha Denman? Was Rappleye's silver-white hair caused by stress, a result of this experienced attorney knowingly defending guilty criminals? Did Marsha scam Rappleye? Why did another attorney appear on the scene?

Attorneys have a way of twisting things like pretzels. In a twisting attempt to trick the judicial system, the court received a letter on November 7, from Thomas A. Warda, a Flint attorney. He requested a motion for a change of venue claiming: *Defendant will not receive a fair trial in Jackson County due to local prejudice against her, as a significant number of alleged victims are Jackson County residents, and because the case is highly publicized in the Jackson County area.* He mentioned Marsha's health problems: lupus, sarcoidosis and others.

In a summary of the argument he stated that his client would be denied her constitutional right to raise a defense if she is not permitted to withdraw her plea, and that none of the theories of criminal law would be served by punishing her for something she did not do. (The Michigan plea withdrawal law provides that a plea must be entered prior to sentencing.)

In a motion to dismiss case he said: *Defendant is charged with violating MCL 750. 218-B.* (This is not listed in the Michigan code.)

He entered a Demand for Discovery requesting: *Police reports, records, statements, documents and materials confiscated by the police, invoice statements and materials from Travel Agents International, all witness reports and exculpatory evidence.*

A statement, *'I am not guilty of the crimes charged against me'* was signed by Marsha L. Denman.

It was Friday, November tenth. I was in a crowd, but alone in my thoughts, waiting for another day in court. It was as though my name had been engraved on the second row bench. It was like the second act of a lousy play.

Brad, Marsha's only support person, smiled at me, offered a friendly, "Hi," and sat alone on the front row. Kathy Hurst took a seat next to me for the Argument on Motions hearing brought about by a surprising event in the Marsha Denman story.

Marsha was dressed for the occasion, in the same wardrobe as before, black skirt and jacket, purple blouse. It appeared that her family knew what would take place and chose to stay away. The news media included TV Channels 2, 6, 10, 12, The *Flint Journal* and a *Jackson Citizen Patriot* newspaper reporter, Scott Davis.

Attorney Warda was short, young and neatly dressed in beige trousers and a navy jacket that accented his wide shoulders. He rubbed his thick black hair and adjusted his gold-rimmed glasses. He and Marsha sat in front of me. He leaned over and whispered in her ear, "Don't answer any questions."

The action began at eight-thirty. Warda stood and made a motion to vacate plea, saying it was wrong regarding justice; that the defendant was to appear on November 15. He said Tabbey told him to try to schedule a motion.

Hurst began by objecting to Warda's request. "If Warda wants to come down to Jackson from Flint, he needs to rely on the court file instead of a conversation with a prosecutor. He's got to do some work on this case," he said.

A man in the front row (probably an assistant because a co-counsel had not been documented) handed Warda a black note-book. He scanned the pages, paced the floor and declared, "If this is to be a trial by ambush—" laughter in the courtroom was so obvious that Ken, the bailiff, stood and said if there was any more outburst he would "clear the court." Order resumed.

Judge Nelson conferred with the clerk who gave Warda a copy of the two alternative sentences that had been provided. Marsha sat quietly holding her chin with one hand as the judge said that sentencing had taken place and he knew at this point, which sentence was going to be effective.

Warda stated that Marsha's former attorney said, in the presence of Marsha and her sister, if she pled no contest she would be given a six months sentence with a jail term held under advisement, or suspended, because of her health conditions. He felt she should be offered an evidentiary hearing to prove whether there had been a promise of leniency.

The judge looked at the newly appointed attorney and again explained that he didn't promise any agreement regarding sentencing and that Marsha was fully advised at the time of the plea.

In another last-ditch effort to get her off the hook, Warda looked at Marsha, played on Judge Nelson's sympathy by imploring, "We're dealing with someone who has never had any dealings with the criminal justice system before. She's got no prior record. She's very scared. She's a sick woman.

"When her attorney said she should plea to the charge, she was unfamiliar with procedures and she was promised no jail time. I think it's logical for that person to say, sure, I'll take whatever deal you give me as long as I don't have to go to jail. I think that's the whole essence of a no contest plea. She informs me to this day, that she maintains her innocence, so at the very least, we would ask for an evidentiary hearing. If Ms. Denman cannot prove that it's reasonable belief that she was given this promise of leniency, then maybe the plea should stand.

"The prosecution knows I'm brand new on this file. I haven't seen any discovery. I've reviewed this for only two days before being here, so I'm at a disadvantage. The defendant is at a disadvantage. She feels she's been mistreated. If the court doesn't want to vacate her plea, at least allow her a hearing.

"This is a very serious charge, a charge of false pretenses as far as I understand. I haven't seen the statute under which the prosecutor is relying, but apparently the prosecutor has a lot of documentary evidence to make these allegations and bring this charge. If that's true then they had no prejudice in being able to present this at this time," he pleaded.

Warda approached the job meticulously like a law student preparing for a final. He pointed out a case that addressed a similar issue and pleaded for a hearing to bare it out whether the defendant was promised leniency, and whether or not she understood exactly what she was doing and what she was getting into. He said, "She never indicated the factual basis to the court indicating her guilt, so we don't have her own statements to deal with."

The blond clerk watched attentively as Judge Nelson calmly explained that the money had not been received, that he had looked at the facts and was satisfied that there was a factual basis.

Marsha sat with her feet crossed, arms leaning on the chair. She appeared to be isolated, like the little girl in a fairy tale who learned she wasn't a princess. Her complexion was fair and neutral. Mr. Warda looked into the observer's section. He and Marsha joined together like drops of water, as the judge read his prepared speech saying there's no reason to appeal.

Warda continued to argue. "According to the police report, and that's only one side of the story, the defendant maintains her innocence here today and none of the witnesses have died or are not to be found. This isn't a case that has lasted for years. If the prosecutor does have this bundle of evidence against the defendant, there should be no prejudice in presenting that evidence." He said that obviously he had been misinformed as to what occurred, apologized for being a neophyte on the files, and pleaded again, "Please, grant an evidentiary hearing."

Hurst gave a rebuttal to the request. His expressions mirrored disgust that this defendant wouldn't face up to her crime. Marsha maintained her self-delusion that she had done nothing wrong, even in the face of overwhelming evidence. There was no crack in the stone wall of denial.

But the swinging gate on my left provided entry for Jackson County Sheriff Deputy, Gregg Pond. The shackles he carried clanked like the shocking blow of prison doors. He stationed himself next to Hurst, who looked dignified in a dark suit, white shirt, red and black striped tie.

Hurst began a powerful summation of his positive opinion. "I'd like to correct Mr. Warda's suggestions to the court that he was unaware that this defendant had been sentenced, by referring to the People's response to the defendant's motion to withdraw plea, which indicated that the sentence had already been imposed by this court. It indicated the terms of the sentence, and if she was unable to pay restitution, she was to report to this court to be transported to prison to begin her sentence.

"Mr. Warda apologizes for the fact that he is a neophyte on this file. That's not the court's responsibility for Ms. Denman to come in here with a new attorney at the last minute, who admits on the record that he is not familiar with this case.

"There were no promises made by this court or the prosecuting attorney. This was a no-deal case. She pled on the nose. There's no affidavit provided by Mr. Warda regarding to the claims of the sister. I reviewed the video sentencing tape and it indicated that we have come long and far enough with this defendant. And further, I think the most significant thing that can take place here would be for Mr. Warda to have his name added to the latest list of Marsha Denman's victims!"

Hurst reminded me of *Matlock* on television, convincing the jury of guilt when he said, in a harsh, gruff manner, "Ms. Denman has what is known as selective recall. At the sentencing hearing, she apologized to this court." He paused, pointed to the observers' section. "And to the victims. She said, 'Your Honor, the restitution will be paid.' The date has past and it's not paid and now it's time for Marsha Denman to be held accountable and responsible for her actions." Pounding his fist on the podium and keeping time with each word, he declared, "And that means time to go to prison."

Warda tried again. "If I may respond, the prosecution has indicated that Marsha Denman has not provided any affidavit—"

Hurst loudly interrupted. "I didn't say that." The judge ignored the outburst.

Warda continued, "My office has filed a two-page affidavit, signed by a notary, where she indicates exactly what she plans on showing at evidentiary hearing, that she was promised leniency. We are entitled to a hearing," he concluded.

The judge rubbed his forehead. "Mr. Warda, I'll overlook a formal order for substitution. Sentencing has occurred. There's no error in the plea. It seems to me that this is a collateral attack upon the plea and sentence as opposed to a direct appeal, which is really what the recourse is at this stage. We need a closure, a finality on this matter, on behalf of the People and the victims."

Judge Nelson reiterated that the court had ordered $200,000 to be paid by November 8, to be held in a trust fund for distribution to the victims. He asked Hurst if he had received the money. Hurst answered that he was sad to say he had not. The judge sighed, and stated, "The alternative sentencing applies. Even today, she continued to deny any wrong doing. There's still a lack of remorse."

The judge had enough. "It was previously revealed to me that Marsha had traveled in Europe. I presume she has a passport. We still have many dollars unaccounted for. There's a substantial reason to fear that she could not show up for sentencing next Wednesday. I hereby revoke the bond and remand her to the custody of the sheriff's department to be returned here next Wednesday for sentencing," he said.

By this time, the defense had little fight left. Warda glanced up as Deputy Pond, with chains palmed, hands folded, stood behind Marsha and waited for the signal to do his job.

Mr. Warda refused to give up. He quickly stood and made another plea. "The defendant was absolutely and totally unprepared—uh, for being incarcerated. She's a sick woman. She doesn't have her medication with her."

The judge continued to write as he assured Warda, "We'll have someone run her medication down or the sheriff's department will get it to her." Tabbey and Hurst stood, shook hands, gathered papers from the desk and placed them in file boxes.

Marsha had fooled Warda, who wasn't completely aware of the situation. I admired his willingness to accept a new case, spending only a few hours to prepare, yet pushing to the limit to get his client off the hook. The deputy moved closer as Warda asked the judge, "She was under the impression that she hasn't been sentenced. How is there such a discrepancy in understandings?"

Judge Nelson ended the day by replying, "You heard my ruling—that's it."

The defense sputtered to a close. Marsha protracted; talked aloud with her attorney. He shook his head. The deputy waited. Marsha stood. At 8:49, Deputy Pond moved closer. Marsha, who appeared to be reserved, extended her arms. The handcuffs clicked. Captivity. Her quiet calmness at the moment he put belly chains around her waist led one to believe that she finally faced reality. Tombstone silence surprised me. No gasping. No tears.

From the back of the courtroom, silent sentries—Siegel and another plain-clothed, off-duty officer—viewed the final investigative results of the Marsha Denman story. The judge stood, closed the window, chatted with the clerk.

I don't know if Marsha saw Brad's tear-filled eyes. He rubbed his hands together as though he didn't know what else to do. Today was the first time I had detected any emotion from Brad, including his salutation to me.

It was a sad day, not that I didn't feel satisfaction, but I remember Marsha's pathetic face, the look of a child who lost her puppy dog. I wondered what was going through her mind. She looked straight ahead as the deputy walked her through the exit door.

The news media and observers dispersed as Siegel and Tabbey cheerfully displayed an Olympic medal grin, energetically shook hands. Some observers shared smiles and a high-five.

Carole France broke into a wide smile that morning, when she saw handcuffs placed on the woman who had swindled her. Out in the noisy hallway, I patted her back and said, "Well, Carole, another chapter is written. How do you feel?"

She answered, "It was wonderful. It was like seeing me take that cruise."

A reporter from CBS waved a microphone in my face. "I have mixed emotions," I said. "I feel pain for others, even if they are guilty. An act of justice closes the book on a misdeed. An act of vengeance writes one of its own."

~ CHAPTER THIRTEEN ~

BEHIND BARS

It was a cold Wednesday, November 15. The leafless trees, crusted overnight with winter ice and snow, made bell-like music as darkness moved into morning. The first glint of a pink sunrise produced brilliant colors, soon turning to yellow-orange as we topped a hill and merged into the traffic on M-60, enroute to the conclusion of the Marsha L. Denman story.

Ken, the bailiff, removed the TV ONLY sign so we took our usual second row seat in the familiar mahogany paneled courtroom. The whoosh of the wooden swinging doors admitted attorneys and reporters. Observers pushed their way into the room to view what we thought would be the last scene in the plot that was cast three years ago.

Marsha's attorney came in, shook hands with Mrs. Denman, who began to cry. Mr. Denman attempted to comfort, patted his wife's back. A deputy accompanied Marsha and a male prisoner into the courtroom. Shackled together by belly chains, their wardrobe consisted of an orange JACKSON COUNTY JAIL jumpsuit, handcuffs and plastic sandals. They shared a nervous smile, took a seat facing the observers. The deputy sat nearby.

A reporter glanced at his watch, looked frustrated, began making notes. The "All rise" command was given as Judge Nelson and his cup of tea swished through the chamber door.

Marsha appeared interested in a case where the defendant's attorney stated his client had paid the requested $100. The judge looked surprised and told the young man, "I didn't think you'd pay—you didn't before—so I'll have to make some new entries." The defendant smiled, displaying white teeth accented by iodine skin, dark eyes. A loose-fitting, wrinkled jacket hung on the man's small lanky form. He tugged at his ear, looked down as he talked, "No suh," he said, "Ah didn't plan to goof up dis time." The audience chortled.

The judge drank tea, smiled often, talked with the clerk while waiting for the next case.

Marsha wore no makeup, but her hair was neatly combed. She sat in the jury chair sometimes rocking back and forth. She appeared to be at ease, indifferent. She and her prisoner partner intermittently talked as though they were old friends. He too, seemed unaffected.

She gave her family an I LOVE YOU hand sign and initiated her second big smile. Mrs. Denman cried. I thought, *How does Marsha feel when she sees those tears she put in her mother's eyes? If I had a mom, I surely wouldn't put tears in her eyes.*

Attorney Warda deliberated with Marsha. We waited. Mr. Denman and Brad looked expressionless, while Lori and Mrs. Denman, who leaned on her cane as though it offered comfort or that it might walk away, fought back tears.

Tabbey casually approached the bench between cases. His spontaneous sense of humor often created a gleam in Judge Nelson's laughing eyes. Kirk Tabbey, the assistant prosecutor who exercised good judgment, tough stance and determination to prosecute offenders, reviewed his notes.

Marsha and her prisoner partner rocked in the chair, shared an uncomfortable smile. During the waiting, Marsha's eyes locked onto Brad's unflinchingly, for a minute or so. She smiled. He returned a buoyant long-lasting one. At the deputy's request,

Marsha shuffled to a seat next to her attorney. The clerk inserted another video tape into the machine. The judge removed his glasses, rubbed his eyes. Tabbey approached the bench. The trio appeared to be in deep conversation until the bailiff announced that "The People vs. Marsha Lee Denman," would begin.

Judge Nelson signed several forms as he recapped the factors of previously provided sentencing, told Marsha that she had a right to appeal within forty-two days. He informed the court that he had recommended to the Department of Corrections that Marsha should not be released from a walled-prison facility for women prior to forty-eight months. No halfway house placement or parole, unless permission was secured from this court. He informed Tabbey that he would sign an order to release the assets that had been frozen and make them available to disburse for restitution.

Warda asked the judge if he would allow allocution, (a chance to apologize). Marsha's mouth contorted into various positions. She scooted around in the seat, turned her head and looked at Warda.

Judge Nelson stated, "We had allocution at the time of sentencing."

"Uh, then, Uh, I'm a little confused on what today would be then, if it's not sentencing."

"We had sentencing previously."

"I understand that."

"I gave you copies of the two sentences. All this was going to do was to see which one was to apply. We had allocution before."

"I understand, may I make a record, Your Honor?"

"On what?"

"On objecting to today's proceeding and objecting to renewing my motion to withdraw her plea."

"Okay. The motion to withdraw the plea is denied. We covered that before."

"Can I quickly make a record?"

"Sure."

"Thank you, Judge," Warda said as he prepared for the last stage of the marathon. He pointed out another case indicating that the plea, using a promise made by the prosecution, was unfulfilled as in this case. The judge continued signing papers while repeating clarification of the facts, stating that the sentencing was totally his decision.

Attorney Warda talked to Marsha for a short time. She returned to the seat in the jury section. He said a few words to the family, stuffed his file into a briefcase. I saw the hurt in Marsha's parents' eyes when they stood and looked around the courtroom that was packed with many of the people Marsha had deceived. As Warda led the family from the room, Mr. Denman looked at Marsha in a warm fatherly fashion and said, "I love you, hon."

Marsha softly replied, "Love you."

Mrs. Denman and her cane ambled along, tears filling her eyes as she uttered," Marsha, I love you." Her daughter appeared unruffled, smiled and echoed the words. Brad's smile lengthened while giving an *I Love You* sign. Marsha returned the gesture, without speaking.

The sound of clanging chains, swaying back and forth, extended the silence as Marsha and her partner, shackled together, walked like umbilicals. I saw a freeze-frame of the rocking. The officer led them to the waiting patrol car, to begin a new chapter in the life of the prisoner who emitted the voice with a smile.

Have we seen the last of Marsha Denman, I wondered as she went through the exit door.

The clerk inserted a new tape, thus beginning another case. Within the walls of this courtroom, the wheels of justice continued to turn.

We crowded into the elevator, pushed the first floor button. Warda dashed in as the door sliced shut. One of the victims broke the silence. "Working for the enemy?"

Warda smiled and said, "Somebody has to do it."

Sgt. Siegel and his friend Sandy joined our large group who celebrated the victory with a Cracker Barrel breakfast and the best cup of coffee in town.

The next day I unfolded the newspaper. The headlines jumped out at me:

TRAVEL AGENT MUST KEEP CABIN ON PRISON CRUISE.

Marsha Denman apparently doesn't like the accommodations that Jackson County Circuit Judge Charles A. Nelson booked for her. The attorney for Denman showed up in court Friday to ask for a better view—something outside the walls of the state prison system. But Nelson said nothing could be done. Reservations have been made. A cell has been booked. And there's no bailing out until the trip is over—in four years.

Marsha's accommodations were booked at the Scott Correctional Facility located on Five Mile Road, Plymouth, Michigan. The facility opened in 1986, employs 330 and houses 862 females in either minimum, medium, or closed security. (Closed security is slightly less severe than maximum.) The daily capacity is 743 convicted felons, housed in unfurnished cells except for a cot, a toilet, a basin, and an overhead light that is never extinguished. The cost is $64.90 per inmate per day.

She was processed and placed in segregation, solitary, to help her become accustomed to confinement, no night life, no distinctive restaurants, far from her previous vacations enjoying a luxurious suite in a posh hotel. Instead, behind cold, steel doors and bars with liars, cheats and common crooks, she will wait for the minutes, hours, months and years to pass. The sameness of prison life is depressing, dangerous and boring. Each inmate is a citizen of a village that exists within the prison's walls.

After four weeks she was placed with the general population. I asked a corrections officer, "Do you have a gender preference regarding where you work?"

He readily answered, "Definitely. Most officers prefer men's facilities. Women prisoners are much more demanding: cosmetics, hair dryers, accessories, as though they dressed for a date each night. They order items through a catalogue and pay direct. **Some** of the male prisoners say they're innocent. **Most** of the females maintain that fact."

"Does Marsha order satin sheets?" I inquired displaying a sarcastic grin.

Marsha spent thirteen months at the Scott Facility. On January 5, 1996, she was transferred to the Florence Crane Facility on Fourth Street in Coldwater, Michigan. The Mental Health Center's six buildings had been renovated to become the Women's Correctional Facility, which houses 460 females aged seventeen and up. The cost per inmate per day is $87. There are 160 corrections officers of a staff numbering 205.

I questioned the reason for transfer. Warden Sally Langley said, "Maybe it was due to over-crowding or because of inmate enemies." Marsha remained at the medium security custody level. If Judge Nelson's sentence is obeyed, the balance of her incarceration will be served in a walled minimum security prison.

I asked Ms. Langley to describe a typical day. "There is no typical day," she said. "A warden comes to work with ideas of accomplishment, but priorities change all day. My day begins with a staff meeting to resolve problems, plan activities. Many days I interact with inmates, often meeting with them on a daily basis, settling grievances. Recently I met with a group of prisoners to talk about the central laundry that was instituted." Sometimes she meets with wardens regarding other institutions and offers help. She receives many calls from prisoners' families regarding visits, health, and other problems.

This facility has open dormitory setting. One unit houses thirty-four inmates and requires one daytime officer. They don't have privacy. The ninety-acre perimeter is covered with electronic monitoring cameras and a 12 foot razor ribbon wire.

All inmates have certain duties working as porters, food service, grounds maintenance and clerk jobs. They arise at six-thirty, eat breakfast at seven-thirty. Some participate in daily physical fitness, but it is not mandatory; 75 percent are involved in the educational program.

A class-action suit filed two decades ago, on behalf of all the state's female inmates, resulted in U.S. District Judge John Feikens ordering the state of Michigan to start providing better apprentice-ship and vocational programs for female inmates at the Scott and Crane Women's Facilities. He ruled that male inmates had far better educational and vocational opportunities than female.

The Corrections Department feels they have exceeded the court's order in providing training programs. The state will have to pay $1,500 a day until it complies. The amount will increase to $15,000 a day if the issues are not addressed within thirty days. John Truscott, a spokesman for Gov. John Engler, feels the order erodes the state's authority to run its prisons.

On November 15, the Collections Manager of the Flint Area School Employees Credit Union notified the prosecuting attorney of the fraudulent transfer of title to the 1994 Pontiac Bonneville on September 26, 1995, the day prior to Marsha's sentencing. The title was transferred to Bradley Younce

Other items identified and described were: $8,492.50 held in the escrow account of TAI; $25.14 in Marsha Denman's Flint School Credit Union account; $5.90 in Marsha Denman's Security Federal Credit Union account; computer, keyboard, monitor, surge pad, surge suppresser, Logitech mouse, DeskJet Printer, diskettes, software and manuals.

These items belong to the victims, and will be sold at public auction and held for distribution to the victims. With final disposition of the case, the prosecuting attorney's office was concerned about the possibility of further fraudulent transfers of illegally converted moneys, therefore, an order was issued that all cash and items received will be forfeited.

I received a letter from the Department of Corrections on December 7. They will look at the judge's letter and consider that Marsha is non-violent. The judge's letter should prevent a tether or parole without his permission. They will keep 108 victims apprised concerning incarceration and release of Marsha Denman, inmate number 246404. The earliest possible date to consider parole is February 1, 1999. It is possible for this date to change due to loss of good time or disciplinary credits, restoration of such lost credits or sentencing amendments.

Perhaps it was because it was December and Christmas activities were in full swing, or maybe it was because I get somewhat sentimental this time of year; but I thought of Marsha, assuming that by now she would be content to deck her 6 by 8 foot cell and make the best of the holiday season. I thought of her promise in court on September 27, and wished that our mail lady would bring a Christmas bonus of $1,450, but lack of faith made me decide to forget about Marsha and move on.

On cold winter mornings, I like to snuggle inside and sleep as late as possible. On December 15, I was awakened by the telephone. My onerous seven o'clock telephone voice managed a friendly response. When I recognized the caller, my first thought was, *My, it's nice that Dennis Hurst is calling to thank me for the Christmas goodies I took to his office last week.* He informed me, "This morning at nine, Marsha's new attorney has scheduled a Motion for Bond Pending Appeal."

It's difficult to make decisions before having my morning coffee, so I scooped out the Folgers® and filled the Bunn® brewer with water. The delicious aroma filled the air, as I began calling those victims who I thought would want to view the action.

We filed into Judge Nelson's courtroom to find Tabbey, Hurst and the Chief Appellate Attorney, Roberta Balon ready and waiting. When three short cases were completed, the judge announced that the People vs. Marsha L. Denman would begin. When I heard those words, I whispered, "Here we go again." Kathy Hurst, Karen Knutson, Lyle and Nancy Sheets, Mel and I occupied front row seats.

Attorney Warda stood. "On behalf of Marsha Denman we have filed a motion requesting bond pending the claim of appeal which we filed on November 27. Both bailable and non-assaultive offenses of false pretense requirements are met and there's an inherent need to protect this defendant. At worst, she's a thief and the majority of victims are from Jackson County where there's a political sentiment to get back at her.

"Many errors prevail. She doesn't have a passport, as the prosecution pointed out. She's never had a passport. She won't flee. It has been a proven fact that she never assaulted anyone. She's thirty-nine and she's sick. It is believed that medications designed to preserve her health are being denied during her incarceration. She won't flee. She will promise in writing to comply. She's signed an affidavit. Defendant prays this Honorable Court to grant an order for bond pending appeal."

Judge Nelson, with ardent compassion for the victims, abruptly stated, "Are we supposed to rely on her word? We've done that time and time again and her word failed." Marsha claimed that her appeal should be granted because she was desperately ill. (Her purported "illness" did not impinge on her numerous travel excursions prior to her arrest.)

Warda protested, "Your Honor, we have an affidavit."

Judge Nelson persisted, "The variation from everyday sentencing procedures was the result of defendant's own request that she be allowed time to pay restitution. The court's sentence merely obliged the defendant in order to allow her to pay restitution owed to, and desperately needed by the victims of her crime. She sent letters to the victims and to the court saying she'd pay. Nothing has happened."

Marsha's claim that she was not afforded her right to allocution at sentencing was without merit. She was properly warned. When I heard her read a prepared statement into the record, I felt she indicated that she had been given all the opportunity for allocution provided by law, and then some. She allocated her own sentence.

Marsha's claim was not a substantial ground for appeal. It was absurd. If her sentence was "disproportionate to the seriousness of the offense and the offender," then it was disproportionate to the detriment of the People. The sentence imposed in this case was clearly proportionate considering the large sums of money taken, the number of victims involved, and the underhanded, manipulative deception perpetrated by Marsha to steal the funds in order to further her lavish lifestyle. To avoid discovery, she conveniently avoided being cross-examined by pleading no contest. I believe this decision was made voluntarily, knowingly, and she had no right to claim otherwise.

Warda advanced his case. "It has already been established regarding the guilt. Her former lawyer dealt with that. How deep does it go? There's an appeal request that can be granted. We're asking for reversal. There have been many errors in this case. We're asking for this decision to be overturned, to withdraw the plea. Sentencing had been adjourned until November 15. There's no Europe, that's not an issue.

"The prosecution says she was already sentenced. An alternative sentence was issued and to say she's already sentenced is an error. We'll set forth an appeal next week. Her doctor says she's sick. The department of corrections says they'll discontinue her medication. The doctor will give a physical to see if she needs medicine. She won't flee. She's not a physical threat. There's only political reasons because of the victims in Jackson County. If she's released, she'll be in Genesee County where there's no threat. She didn't pay off her car," he said.

The judge corrected Warda's statement. "She paid off her bank loan the day before her sentencing."

Warda's voice elevated. "Her husband obtained a loan for $6,000. These allegations are untrue. The statues have been met. She has appeared as scheduled. It's public outcry."

Those who were familiar with the case gasped, displayed a surprise reaction to the word *husband*. Verification with several sources revealed no marriage license had been issued, although there is reason to believe that she was married.

Hurst stuck to the facts. "Mr. Warda is persistent in using his defense, but he's not accurate. There are 573 victims involved and one hundred or so are from Jackson County, many are from Genesee County. There's no political involvement in this case. We want justice. When the State Police showed up for a search warrant, she was at that moment trying to erase evidence.

"We can't allow her to keep coming and asking the court to release her because she doesn't like prison. She should have thought of that before. Ms. Denman isn't going to die in prison. She's not that ill. This woman pled no contest and indicated she knew what she was doing. On September 27, she stood here and declared to the victims how sorry she was, and she promised restitution. If Mr. Warda had reviewed those court video transcripts he would have found that everything is accurate. He would have seen it on the transcript; he can't rely on Marsha Denman's word."

The judge calmly inquired. "If she posted a $350,000 bond would that be sufficient in your mind?"

Hurst endured. He spoke with persuasive assurance. "We would be taking that bond which should belong to the victims. I would consider that as an appeal. I would ask that it be awarded to the victims. In the last two days we have received word from the U.S. District Attorney to prosecute her for the crimes. If she's released she'll be a flight risk. Defendant has made numerous trips to destinations around the United States and Canada using the money she stole from the victims in this case. This is a frivolous plea."

Attorney Warda stood with legs open a bit and one hand on his hip, as if he owned a big mountain, and claimed that Hurst didn't address the fact that she had committed a non-violent offense. He said, "It's allegations by the prosecutors because they don't like Marsha Denman. She was railroaded." A stir that suggested disapproval swept the audience. Victims looked at each other and shook their head in disgust.

Judge Nelson glanced at the audience, removed his glasses, swiveled his chair. He was fed up. He raised his voice a little as he not only clarified the facts, but challenged the accusation that he had failed to do his job. "She was sentenced on September 27. This sentence was intelligently entered into by Ms. Denman. I explained everything to her. She was given the keys to the jailhouse. She has been properly sentenced. I don't see any reason to change it. She's got the money buried somewhere. I don't see any reason to pursue this any further. If you want to appeal, go ahead."

Mr. Warda abruptly hastened to the prosecutor's desk coolly stating, "I'm submitting a Request to Appeal." Ms. Balon, Tabbey, Hurst and Warda approached the judge.

A crowd of victims left the courtroom and stood near the doorway discussing the astonishing new developments in this case. The bailiff, in a reverberating voice, made the announcement that the day in court wasn't over yet and he wouldn't allow interruption. He said if the crowd didn't immediately disperse he would seek action for removal. As Hurst motioned us down the hall, Warda advanced and asked him, "Why don't you like me? Your classmate lawyers told me you're a nice guy."

"I have nothing against you. I just don't like your client," Hurst said with a modest grin.

"This calls for breakfast at Jacobson's," Lyle said as he and Nancy, Mel and I strolled down South Jackson Street. While waiting for the WALK light, I admired the picturesque Christmas decorations and holly garlands. Swags of gala greenery trimmed with gold lighted angels connected the city streets. It was 10:15, and I had just enough time to socialize a bit, then join my friends at the Aerobics Christmas Party.

On Christmas Eve, my alto voice accompanied the excellent sound of Monte Long's choir cantata, *Bethlehem Joy.*

Mel videotaped the holiday vests, red bow ties, glittery green, gold and black dresses. He panned the soloists, flute trio, baby grand piano, and the back row, where Judge Charles Nelson modulated his fine bass voice.

The closing prayer produced silence. The awesome awareness of the holiday spirit lingered until it was interrupted by several babies exercising their lungs, vying for their parents' attention.

As we left, I greeted Judge Nelson. We talked, not about the Denman case, but about the Bethlehem joy we experienced while sharing those few moments of peace on earth.

Outside, luminaria Christmas candles lined the pathway through the heavy snow that surrounded the cozy country church.

~ CHAPTER FOURTEEN ~

THE LAST CHAPTER

It seems only yesterday that we welcomed the arrival of a new year, expecting promise and hope, personal goals and objectives. Then we found ourselves deep into December preparing to usher that month into history. Christmas came and went and we plunged into another year, 1996, with many victims having experienced healing and forgiveness.

My mind replayed the stunning, short-lived dream that transformed into regret that we made a bad choice. As time began to heal, a soft voice from somewhere inside seemed to say: "All of us have made foolish choices and have been hurt by others, but we can't let what we've done in the past or what has been done to us control the choices we make for the future."

It's difficult to understand human behavior. By pleading no contest, Marsha did not admit guilt or innocence before the victims, but if she has faith in God, she will no longer try to manipulate events. Will she be able to deny subterfuge on her part when she reaches the ultimate judgment? Marsha did not reflect good judgment.

The Marsha Denman case is a glaring example of why white collar fraud prosecutions are important. The prosecuting attorney's office established the white collar crime unit in January 1993, with the goal of prosecuting frauds and other white collar crimes. Consumer fraud cases were often ignored or deferred to other agencies, leaving victims in Jackson County without recourse, restitution or justice.

Frauds, con artists, computer criminals, embezzlers and corporate thieves who defraud our residents, employers, local businesses, the Social Security Trust Fund or the welfare system cause significant losses and expense in stolen property.

These crimes force higher prices on all local consumers and reduce the amount of available government benefits or program funds to our citizens, programs designated for the needy, not the greedy. Even more damaging than the higher prices we must all pay because of these criminals is the effect of their crimes on victims, especially the needy, trusting, caring individuals.

American consumers have a new weapon, tough Federal rules, effective January 1, 1996. State attorney generals can now initiate enforcement action through the Federal courts. This grants them the ability to reach schemers wherever they set up shop. They will be able to pursue con artists across state lines.

A high-tech way for crime victims to keep tabs on the criminals who victimized them is being developed in three Michigan counties. The Victim Information and Notification Everyday program will use computers to make sure victims are called when an inmate who has victimized them escapes or is released. Victims also will get information on court hearings. The calling service will provide inmate information around the clock through an automated telephone system. If the pilot project in Wayne, Ingham and Newaygo counties is successful, the program will go statewide.

On January 26, Roberta Balon, Assistant Prosecuting Attorney, sent Dennis Hurst a letter that contained a courtesy notice to be hand-delivered to Bradley Younce. The letter was in reference to the disposition of the 1994 Pontiac Bonneville that was seized by the Michigan State Police pursuant to a court order dated December 5, 1995. The title was to be transferred to the Office of Prosecuting Attorney and the vehicle was to be sold at public auction.

The proceeds of this sale were to be distributed, on a pro rata basis, to the victims of Marsha Denman's criminal activity.

A state trooper delivered the letter on January 30. Bradley was given ten days to seek action, hire an attorney to do so, or it would be assumed that he waived any rights for claim to the vehicle.

There's another twist in the story. Bradley found a lawyer that believed he had the right to keep the vehicle. Tabbey believes the vehicle was the fruits of a fraud; therefore, it belongs to the victims. He said, "The day before Marsha was sentenced, Bradley contacted a bank who, as a good-faith purchaser and without knowledge of what was involved, granted a $10,000 loan on the vehicle. Marsha paid the balance owed, [$6,000] and used the remaining $4,000 to pay her attorney thus gaining more money. As a result, the car has been obligated with a loan and if legal authorities sell the vehicle the bank must be paid first."

The prosecutors had spent many hours attempting to accomplish restitution. Tabbey's work on this and other complicated fraud cases was recognized and effective April 1, 1996, he was promoted to Chief Assistant Prosecuting Attorney. Tabbey enjoys the thought of tackling a new challenge.

To further illustrate his assertion to discipline white collar criminals, on April 2, Tabbey and I attended a press conference in Lansing, led by Kalamazoo's State Representative Charles R. Perricone. Recognizing the need to update Michigan computer fraud laws, Perricone sought out a staff of experts and the Computer Task Force. Several Ameritech technicians using overhead projectors explained the magnitude of computer fraud, visualized prevention, stating that most telephone fraud is committed by prisoners.

Tabbey and I spoke on behalf of victims. I pointed out, "Computer technology was used to perpetrate the travel scam. The process of sending up to twenty pieces of mail to each household using a typewriter and printing service, would have been costly.

"When the cruise date changed, Ms. Denman she had only two days to send information to 573 victims. I feel that the typewriter could not have accomplished the task unless several people were involved, people who would testify in court. With a computer, she was able to quickly encourage the victims to accept the special cabin upgrade offer."

As a result of Perricone's efforts, the bills propelled almost unanimously through the House of Representatives and unanimously through the Senate. Its passage will decrease the number of victims involved and prosecute the guilty.

In an effort to increase the public's awareness and support of victims' rights, I was asked to share my experience as a victim of crime and participate in the program, *A New Day Dawns*. This event commemorated the 1996 National Crime Victims' Rights Week. Victims were inspired and given hope.

Robert and Helene DeMain were unable to attend the program. They wrote a "Thank you" in the March 14, *Jackson Citizen Patriot*, Voice of the People column.

> As one of many victims of the vacation scam perpetrated by Marsha Denman, we [sic] would like to express our appreciation to your prosecuting attorney, Dennis Hurst, and his fine staff for their work on our behalf. We were very pleased with the thorough research and aggressive prosecution of the case. They kept us updated as events developed and sent us copies of all pertinent information.
>
> We were also most impressed with the Victim Rights Unit. . . . They were thorough in carrying out their responsibilities.
>
> It is our opinion that the people of Jackson are fortunate to have a prosecutor who appears to be capable and efficient in carrying out the duties of his office. It seems as though your tax dollars are being well spent.

Truly, the Jackson office's loss of a capable and efficient prosecutor was Washtenaw County's gain. On April 11, 1997, a large group of family, friends and colleagues witnessed Kirk Tabbey's oath to carry out the duties of District Judge. His mother gave him a gavel, along with her blessing and a big hug. By expertness of knowledge, Tabbey is certainly qualified to hear and pass judgment, and has the ability to understand the victims' situation.

Crime victims would be given broad new rights to collect financial restitution and track the status of cases under legislation being drafted by the Clinton administration.

On April 16, a multimillion-dollar victim notification system, similar to the pilot project developed in Michigan, was the center-piece of a package outlined by Attorney General Janet Reno. Under this legislation, crime victims would be given broad new rights to track the status of cases and collect financial restitution. Such an amendment would ensure that crime victims are at the center of the criminal justice process, not on the outside looking in.

Do you believe Marsha is guilty of planning a fraudulent act? Does she have the victims' money? Does Sarah Daws exist? Do you believe, after all, that Marsha is innocent? I do not pass my views upon you as if they were Gospel. I took my text from what occurred in the courtroom. I gave the facts as I saw them, so you can make up your mind as to the guilt. As we would have heard in a jury trial, "Ladies and gentlemen, the verdict is yours."

The last chapter of the Marsha L. Denman story has not been written. Even so, we must not keep smashed dreams alive. Rec-onciliation denotes breaking down walls and forgiving. We must never relive frustration and nurture the bitterness it left in our minds, but let it settle to the bottom of our memories. We don't have time to allow bitterness to control us. We've got one shot at life.

I previously mentioned Glen Siefken, our friend who had a fatal heart attack when Marsha's empire collapsed. The last time we talked, I asked, "Is everything fine?"

He replied, as he had on numerous occasions, "Copasetic, wonderful." Now, he looks down from another place—perhaps asking the question, "Marsha, is everything copasetic?"

Sometimes the end is just the beginning, an unopened door. You don't know about it until you walk through it. I've scheduled an Alaskan cruise for next year, at an *unbelievable* price. I happen to have ten more openings if you'd like to invite some friends. From the beginning to the end, it's going to be an adventure!